CONTENTS

committee has drawn conclusions relating to the health effects of both active and passive smoking and has made recommendations based on those conclusions. However, we felt that it was vital to focus on key messages, for individuals and for government, which appear at the beginning of the report. These key messages address the topics of active smoking, passive smoking, nicotine addiction, price and marketing of tobacco products and smoking cessation.

With your consent, we sought expert opinions on advertising of tobacco products, particularly in relation to vulnerable young people. We share your concern that the prevalence of cigarette smoking is rising in schoolchildren and welcome the consensus achieved by European Health Ministers on banning tobacco advertising.

If we are to reduce the predicted mortality from tobacco related diseases, amongst our current smokers, then we feel that there should be particular focus on smoking cessation interventions by health professionals and increased utilisation of the effective nicotine medications by smokers who are motivated to stop.

It is salutary to note that one third of the cancer deaths in Britain and one sixth of deaths from other causes could be prevented by avoidance of smoking. If we are serious about improving public health then tobacco control warrants priority attention from government. Resources devoted to this area should reap substantial benefits for the current generation of smokers and for generations to come.

I would like to thank the members of my committee for their invaluable support, expertise and patience. I would also like to extend my gratitude to the medical and scientific secretariat for their hard work and enthusiasm.

Yours sincerely

David Poswillo

Chairman

Copies to :
Sir David Carter CMO Scotland
Dr Ruth Hall   CMO Wales
Dr Henrietta Campbell   CMO Northern Ireland

INTRODUCTION

Much is known about the harmful effects of tobacco on health: overall about half of all persisting regular cigarette smokers are killed by tobacco. Even so many people continue to smoke and in 1996 in England 28% of adults were regular cigarette smokers[1] and still about 30% of all deaths in middle age are caused by the habit. To ensure progress in the area of tobacco control and to inform future action, there is a need to keep under review up to date medical, scientific and behavioural information in this area, and therefore, in 1994, the Department of Health (DH) established the Scientific Committee on Tobacco and Health (SCOTH). SCOTH, assisted by the Technical Advisory Group (TAG), embarked on a programme of scientific review and appraisal of a range of important issues related to tobacco and health. This Report to the Chief Medical Officer describes the matters considered by the Committee. The topics addressed were diverse and wide ranging, and they consequently vary in their implications for public health.

THE STRUCTURE OF THE REPORT

Since the inaugural meeting in March 1994, the Committee has received a number of presentations on issues relevant to tobacco and health, has considered contemporary publications, and has reviewed DH commissioned studies. In general, the Committee met four times a year.

The Report opens with *key messages*, to which members wish to give particular prominence. The key messages are followed by the Committee's conclusions and recommendations, for each individual part of the report, which are drawn together for ease of reference.

The main body of the Report begins with a global view of the scale of the smoking problem **(Part One)**. In this section the evolving tobacco epidemic in less developed countries is contrasted with that of the developed world. The situation in the United Kingdom is described. The section considers nicotine addiction and finishes with a brief overview of smoking-related diseases and their attributable risks.

The main topic under consideration by SCOTH has been the health effects of exposure of non-smokers to environmental tobacco smoke (ETS), in particular the evaluation of possible increased risks of lung cancer, ischaemic heart disease, and respiratory and other diseases in childhood. The Committee considered new overviews in these three areas, commissioned by DH, and also received papers on ETS and lung cancer from the Tobacco Manufacturers' Association. The Committee was assisted in their deliberations on ETS and lung cancer by a statement from the Committee on Carcinogenicity of Chemicals in Food, Consumer Products and the Environment (CoC). **Part Two** of the report addresses these topics.

Part Three of the report examines general aspects of the influence of price and promotion on tobacco consumption. Given the concern about the increasing prevalence of smoking in young people, the Committee considered DH commissioned work on factors relevant to adolescent smoking and heard presentations on the effect of advertising on young people. This aspect is dealt with in **Part Four.**

The important area of smoking cessation and the role of nicotine replacement therapy is considered in **Part Five**.

Miscellaneous topics are described in **Part Six** of the report, which includes the effect of smoking on performance and mood, smoking in pregnancy and congenital defects, oral cancer and periodontal disease, and diseases with a lower risk in smokers.

At each meeting the Committee was updated on the activities of the Technical Advisory Group (TAG), mentioned in **Part Seven** of the report, which also deals with the routine and research programme of the Laboratory of the Government Chemist (LGC). The specific work of the TAG to review emissions from cigarette smoke is included in **Part Seven**.

Part Eight explains the revised Voluntary Agreement for the approval of new additives to tobacco products.

Part Nine takes a brief look at areas of interest which require more research or in which new developments are to be expected.

Separate annexes **(Annexes A-G)** at the end of the report include information on the previous Independent Scientific Committee on Smoking and Health (ISCSH), and the Terms of Reference and Membership of SCOTH and TAG.

KEY MESSAGES

1   ACTIVE SMOKING

Smoking is a major cause of illness and death from cardiovascular disease, chronic respiratory disease and cancer of the lung and other sites. It is the most important cause of premature death in developed countries and accounts for one fifth of all deaths in the UK: some 120,000 deaths a year.[2]

The avoidance of smoking would prevent one third of the deaths due to cancer in Britain and one sixth of the deaths from other causes. A person who smokes cigarettes regularly, more than doubles his or her risk of dying before the age of 65, and half of all who continue to smoke cigarettes are eventually killed by the habit,[3] but stopping smoking is effective: even in middle age those who stop before they have overt disease avoid most of their risk of death from tobacco, and for those who stop before middle age the benefits are even greater.

The enormous damage to health and the large number of deaths caused by smoking should no longer be accepted. The Government should take effective action to limit this preventable epidemic.   The importance and urgency of the smoking problem needs to be recognised by both the Government and the public.

The Government should require of the tobacco industry a normal standard of disclosure and the recognition of the evidence that smoking is a major cause of premature death. Tobacco manufacturers should be required to inform their customers clearly and accurately of the nature and magnitude of the risks of smoking.

2   PASSIVE SMOKING

Passive smoking is a cause of lung cancer and childhood respiratory disease. There is also evidence that passive smoking is a cause of ischaemic heart disease and cot death, middle ear disease and asthmatic attacks in children.   Restrictions on smoking in public places and work places are necessary to protect non smokers. Parents need to be informed about the effects of passive smoking on their children.

3   NICOTINE ADDICTION

Addiction to nicotine is now known to sustain the smoking epidemic. Thirty five years after the first report by the Royal College of Physicians on Smoking and Health, nearly 30% of adults in the UK still smoke. Smoking in young adults is on the increase, leading to an overall rise in adult smoking prevalence in 1996 after 24 years of steady decline. Most smokers begin in their teenage years, at a time when the prospect of illness and death in adult life seems remote. Some eventually give up the habit, but for many the intractability of smoking behaviour reflects the fact that nicotine is a powerful drug of addiction.

4   PRICE AND ADVERTISING

Price and marketing are important factors in influencing cigarette consumption. Regular price increases above inflation will reduce consumption. Young people in particular should not be exposed to tobacco advertising or to the images associated with sports promotion and other forms of indirect advertising. These counteract public health messages, undermine a proper understanding of the real size of the hazard and promote the social acceptability of cigarette smoking. In view of the burden of disease and death caused by tobacco, there can no longer be any justification for the deliberate promotion of this habit, which is the most important cause of cancer in the world.

5   SMOKING CESSATION

Because of the time lag before onset of morbidity, the prospects for reducing smoking related disease in the next 20 years depend mainly on increasing the rate at which established smokers give up the habit. Policies to increase the price of cigarettes and to restrict smoking in public places are effective in encouraging many to quit, but smokers often find it difficult to overcome their dependence without help. Effective treatments to promote smoking cessation are available and need to be implemented in primary care, hospitals, pharmacies and other health settings.

SUMMARY OF CONCLUSIONS AND RECOMMENDATIONS

THE SCALE OF THE SMOKING PROBLEM (PART ONE) _____

Conclusions:

Smoking is a major cause of illness and death from chronic respiratory diseases, cardiovascular disease, and cancers of the lung and other sites.

Smoking is the most important cause of premature death in developed countries. It accounts for one fifth of deaths in the UK: some 120,000 deaths a year.

The avoidance of smoking would eliminate one third of the cancer deaths in Britain and one sixth of the deaths from other causes.

Smoking prevalence in young people rose between 1988 and 1997 and the downward trend in adult smoking, noted in the UK since 1972, was reversed in 1996.

A person who smokes cigarettes regularly more than doubles his or her risk of dying before the age of 65.

Addiction to nicotine sustains cigarette smoking and is responsible for the remarkable intractability of smoking behaviour.

Smoking in pregnancy causes adverse outcomes, notably an increased risk of miscarriage, reduced birth weight and perinatal death. If parents continue to smoke after pregnancy there is an increased rate of sudden infant death syndrome.

Cigarette smoking is an important contributor to health inequalities, being much more common amongst the disadvantaged than the affluent members of society.

Recommendations:

The enormous damage to health and life arising from smoking should no longer be accepted; the Government should take effective action to limit this preventable epidemic.

The Government should require of the tobacco industry:

    a. reasonable standards in the assessment of evidence relating to the health effects of the product it sells,

    b. acceptance that smoking is a major cause of premature death, and

c.   normal standards of disclosure of the nature and magnitude of the hazards of smoking to their customers, comparable to that expected from other manufacturers of consumer products.

Independently of specific governmental regulations, tobacco manufacturers should comply with these requirements.

There is an importance and urgency with the smoking problem that needs to be recognised by both the Government and the public.

ENVIRONMENTAL TOBACCO SMOKE (PART TWO)

Conclusions:

Exposure to environmental tobacco smoke is a cause of lung cancer and, in those with long term exposure, the increased risk is in the order of 20-30%.

Exposure to environmental tobacco smoke is a cause of ischaemic heart disease and, if current published estimates of magnitude of relative risk are validated, such exposure represents a substantial public health hazard.

Smoking in the presence of infants and children is a cause of serious respiratory illness and asthmatic attacks.

Sudden infant death syndrome, the main cause of post-neonatal death in the first year of life, is associated with exposure to environmental tobacco smoke. The association is judged to be one of cause and effect.

Middle ear disease in children is linked with parental smoking and this association is likely to be causal.

Recommendations:

Smoking in public places should be restricted on the grounds of public health. The level of restriction should vary according to the different categories of public place but smoking should not be allowed in public service buildings or on public transport, other than in designated and isolated areas.   Wherever possible, smoking should not be allowed in the work place.

There is a need for public education about the risks of smoking in the home particularly in relation to respiratory diseases in children.

Health education programmes should focus on the dangers of ETS in fetal development and, postnatally, in the sudden infant death syndrome.

THE INFLUENCE OF PRICE AND PROMOTION ON TOBACCO CONSUMPTION (PART THREE)

Conclusions:

Price, advertising and promotion influence tobacco consumption.

Prevalence of smoking in the United Kingdom is increasingly associated with factors of social and economic deprivation.

Recommendations:

The real price of tobacco products should continue to be increased each year to reduce consumption.

All forms of tobacco advertising, promotion and identifiable sponsorship should be banned.

SMOKING AND YOUNG PEOPLE (PART FOUR)

Conclusions:

Targeting of young people by tobacco companies is of particular relevance because of the now acknowledged addictive nature of tobacco.

Price, advertising and promotion influence cigarette consumption among young people.

Interventions to prevent smoking in young people should form part of concerted action involving all agencies including home, school, community and Government.

Recommendations:

Young people, in particular, should be protected by a ban on all forms of tobacco advertising and promotion.

The real price of tobacco products should continue to be increased each year to discourage young people from smoking.

Changes in smoking prevalence in younger age groups should be monitored.

Educating young people about tobacco addiction and its effects on health should remain an important part of the school curriculum.

Young people themselves should be involved in looking at constructive ways of reducing initiation of smoking.

SMOKING CESSATION (PART FIVE)

Conclusions:

There is evidence that advice on smoking cessation from health care professionals is effective and worthwhile.

Nicotine replacement offers a useful and effective adjunct to advice and increases cessation rates.

Nicotine Replacement Therapy has not been evaluated in pregnancy.

Recommendations:

Smoking cessation interventions by health care professionals are worthwhile and should be encouraged.

The timing and nature of advice provided by doctors and midwives to pregnant smokers should be standardised and the effectiveness of such measures should be evaluated.

Nicotine Replacement Therapy is recommended to reduce withdrawal symptoms and improve cessation rates in smokers who are motivated to give up.

Consideration should be given to ways of increasing the availability of NRT products including via General Sales List and National Health Service prescriptions.

A randomised controlled trial is needed on the efficacy and safety of nicotine replacement therapy for pregnant women who smoke heavily and are unable to give up smoking with current advice and support.

Research is needed on the efficacy and safety of the long term use of NRT as a harm-reduction agent for smokers unable to quit.

THE EFFECT OF SMOKING ON COGNITIVE PERFORMANCE AND MOOD (PART SIX - 6.1)

Conclusions:

In habitual smokers nicotine does not appear to enhance performance above non-smoker levels.

In spite of widespread perceptions to the contrary, stress and anxiety are reduced rather than increased after giving up smoking.

The evidence that smoking relieves stress is weak; rather the reverse is true.

Recommendations:

The public should be made aware of the association between smoking and negative mood states.

SMOKING AND CANCERS OF THE MOUTH AND PHARYNX (PART SIX - 6.2)

Conclusions:

Many cancers of the mouth and pharynx are caused by smoking tobacco and drinking excessive amounts of alcohol, the effect of the two factors together being greater than the sum of each alone.

Oral cancer, in particular, can be easily detected and early treatment is successful.

Recommendations:

The National Screening Committee should consider screening programmes for the early detection of cancers in the mouth.

Mandatory training and updating courses, in the detection of oral cancers, should be organised for dental surgeons and dental hygienists.

Consideration should be given to the re-introduction of dental health checks.

Health education should include information about the increased risk in smokers of these cancers.

THE EFFECT OF SMOKING ON TOOTH LOSS (PART SIX - 6.3)

Conclusions:

Smoking plays a major part in the development of periodontitis, which is the major cause of tooth loss.

Smoking masks the early warning signs of the disease.

Dental surgeons and dental hygienists can play an important role in providing information to the general public on known health risks of smoking including those associated with dental disease.

Recommendations:

The public should be made aware of the role of smoking in the development of gum disease and subsequent tooth loss.

Dentists and dental hygienists should be trained in smoking cessation techniques and encouraged to play an active part in smoking cessation and health education on known health risks of smoking including those associated with dental disease.

SMOKING AND CONGENITAL DEFECTS (PART SIX - 6.4)

Conclusion:

Maternal smoking in pregnancy may increase the risk of congenital defects. Prevention may require smoking cessation before conception.

Recommendations:

The public should be kept aware of the known hazards of smoking in pregnancy.

Further research on smoking in pregnancy and congenital defects is needed.

DISEASES WITH LOWER RISKS IN SMOKERS (PART SIX - 6.5)

Conclusion:

The health benefits of active smoking in a few conditions are far outweighed by the substantial risks.

Recommendation:

The apparent beneficial effects of smoking on a few aspects of health offer an opportunity for research on the mechanisms involved, and the possibilility of developing new pharmaceutical approaches to treatment.

THE REVIEW OF EMISSIONS FROM CIGARETTES (PART SEVEN)

Conclusions:

Reduction in tar yields has contributed modestly to reduction in mortality from some diseases caused by smoking, particularly lung cancer.

Tar reduction is no substitute for not smoking since even low tar cigarettes continue to carry important health risks.

The yields of tar, nicotine, some N-nitroso compounds and carbon monoxide from hand-rolled cigarettes are higher on average than those from manufactured cigarettes.

Nicotine has been shown conclusively to be addictive.

Recommendations:

A policy of further tar reductions in manufactured cigarettes should be pursued without compromising the message of the importance of not smoking.

As a consequence of potential tar reductions, and thus changes to the manufacturing processes, the monitoring of tar, nicotine and carbon monoxide levels should continue. There should also be investigation into changes in harmful compounds as manufacturing processes change.

The public should be made aware of the relatively high yields of harmful compounds in hand rolled cigarettes and of their potential impact on health.

There is a continuing need for population studies, such as the Health Survey for England, which relate tobacco type and yield, smoking behaviour and intake and the incidence and prevalence of tobacco related diseases.

Consideration should be given to smoking status being recorded as part of the death registration process, to aid monitoring of the evolving epidemic of tobacco related diseases.

VOLUNTARY AGREEMENT FOR THE APPROVAL OF NEW ADDITIVES TO TOBACCO PRODUCTS (PART EIGHT)

Recommendations:

The use of additives in tobacco products should continue to be closely monitored.

The Technical Advisory Group should regularly review the changing patterns and types of additives.

PART ONE

THE SCALE OF THE SMOKING PROBLEM

A Global Overview

1.1   Tobacco is the single most important avoidable cause of chronic ill health and premature death in developed countries, where it now causes a quarter of all the deaths in middle age, with maximum mortality among males and rising mortality among females. In developing countries many men now smoke, and mortality from tobacco is increasing. Worldwide, if current smoking patterns persist, then annual tobacco deaths will increase from 3 million in the early 1990s (10% of all adult deaths) to 10 million by the late 2020s.[4]

1.2   The Health Education Authority (HEA) recently estimated that there were 120,000 deaths attributable to smoking in 1995 in the United Kingdom.[2] The British Regional Heart Study reported that men who have never smoked have a 78% chance of reaching 73 years of age whereas those who start smoking by the age of 20 and never stop have only a 42% chance.[5] The 40 year prospective study of male British doctors, started in 1951, indicated that the hazards of prolonged tobacco use are greater than was thought to be the case 20 years ago.[6] Figure 1, based on the whole study, shows the effects on survival to age 70 and to age 85.[3] The evidence since 1971 indicates almost a three-fold difference in mortality during middle age between smokers and non-smokers.

1.3   A UK study of over 10,000 survivors from heart attacks, published in August 1995, showed that smokers in their thirties and forties have five times as many heart attacks as non-smokers.[7] (Figure 2)

1.4   In Great Britain, there was a reduction in the number of adult cigarette smokers (aged 16 and over) from 45% of the population in 1974 to 27% in 1994 but an increase to 28% in 1996[1] The decline has been confined to adults aged 35 and over. There has been little change since the early 1980s in smoking prevalence in children aged under 16 years, but the 1996 Office for National Statistics' (ONS) figures showed an increase. (See para. 1.19 below). The smoking habit is initiated in the early teens and by the age of 16 a third of all young people, male or female, are smoking at least one cigarette a week. A major trend in many developed countries is the rise in deaths caused by smoking among women. In Scotland lung cancer has overtaken breast cancer as the leading cause of female death from malignant disease, and the same has happened in North America.

1.5   In the United States tobacco use kills more than 400,000 people each year. This figure is more than the *combined* deaths each year from AIDS, car accidents, alcohol, homicides, illegal drugs, suicides and fires.[8] It has been estimated that on average, of one thousand 20 year olds in the United States who smoke cigarettes regularly, about six will die from homicide, about 12 from motor vehicles, about 250 will be killed by smoking in middle age and another 250 in old age.[3]   The same estimation of current average risks for one thousand UK 20 year olds who smoke cigarettes regularly is that about one will   die   from   homicide,   six   from   motor   vehicles   and

Figure 1*:   Effect of cigarette smoking on survival to age 70 and to age 85, in 40-year prospective study of male British doctors Source: Doll, Peto et al, 1994

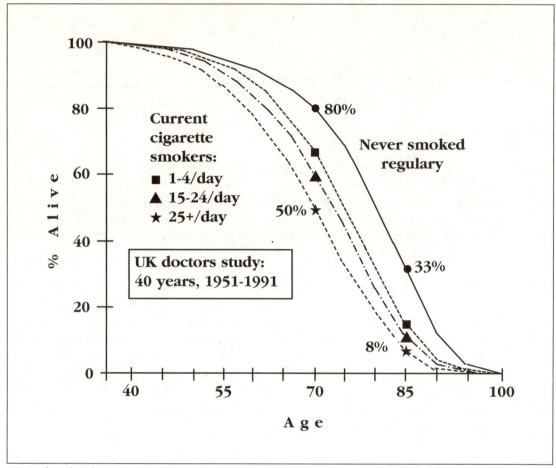

*Reproduced with permission.

Figure 2*:   Ratio of heart attack rates: U.K. smokers vs. non-smokers of the same age

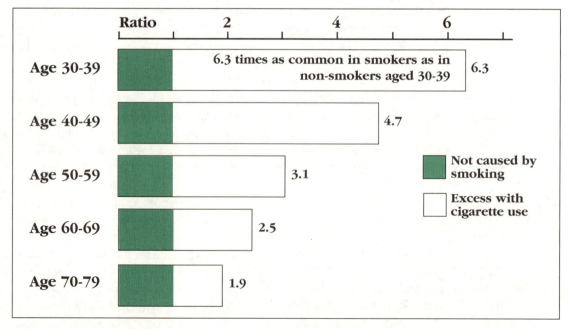

*Reproduced with permission.

250 will be killed by smoking in middle age and 250 in old age.[3] (Middle age is defined as 35 to 69 years).

1.6   There is estimated to be over a billion smokers in the world today, with almost one third of them living in China. The number of cigarettes consumed per adult each year in China rose from 700 in 1970 to 2000 in 1990/92 (almost all of which are smoked by men.). By 1985 sales of cigarettes had doubled over 30 years in a number of developed countries. Tobacco consumption has also increased in certain European countries (France, Germany, Austria, Denmark, Sweden, Greece, Italy, Spain and Portugal) and in Japan[9] but has decreased in others (United Kingdom, Finland, The Netherlands, Switzerland) and in Australia, Canada, and North America.

1.7   Cigarettes were responsible for about 1.2 million deaths in the European Region of the World Health Organisation in 1995, almost three quarters of a million of which occurred in middle age (35 - 69 years).[3]   The percentage of male deaths attributable to smoking is substantial everywhere, with the highest proportions in Central and Eastern Europe. Among women, the percentage varies more widely, being high in the UK but very low in countries where the increase in female smoking is only recent.

1.8   The British Medical Bulletin on Tobacco and Health,[9] published in 1996, estimated the number of deaths attributable to smoking in forty developed countries and calculated that in 1990 smoking accounted for 35% of all deaths in middle aged males (35-69 years of age). In a monograph[3] published in 1994, Peto and others calculated that the average loss of life expectancy for all cigarette smokers in the developed world who die from smoking related diseases is about 16 years. For those who die in middle age (35-69 years) the figure is 22 years and for those killed by tobacco at older ages the figure is 8 years. The proportion of female deaths in middle age that are attributable to tobacco is now approaching the male figure in many countries where women have smoked cigarettes regularly for several decades. The large increases in numbers of women smoking in countries such as France, the Netherlands and Spain are expected to result in substantial rises in female mortality early in the next century.

1.9   The increasing prevalence of smoking in third world countries and in eastern Europe is expected to give rise to increasing numbers of deaths worldwide in the early decades of the next century. It is difficult to give precise figures but, if current smoking patterns persist, the current estimate of three million deaths annually in the world as a whole is likely to rise to 10 million a year in about 30 years' time.[3]

1.10   Many poor countries have seen increasing male tobacco consumption and limited regulatory measures. For example, the US Centres for Disease Control and Prevention show smoking has risen in sub-Saharan Africa where cheap brands are available and tobacco companies are using intensive advertising and marketing campaigns, sponsorship of events and cigarette price wars. (Lancet 13.9.97)

The Health of the Nation

1.11   In 1992, the previous Government's white paper entitled The Health of the Nation[10] set a National Target for England to reduce the death rate from lung cancer in people under the age of 75 by at least 30% in men and at least 15% in women by 2010 (Baseline 1990). There were four additional targets for reduction of risk factors:

i   to reduce the prevalence of cigarette smoking in men and women aged 16 and over to no more than 20% by the year 2000 (a reduction of at least 35% in men and 29% in women, from prevalences in 1990 of 31% and 28% respectively);

ii   in addition to the overall reduction in prevalence, at least a third of women smokers to stop smoking at the start of their pregnancy by the year 2000;

iii   to reduce the consumption of cigarettes by at least 40% by the year 2000 (from 98 billion manufactured cigarettes per year in 1990 to 59 billion);

iv   to reduce smoking prevalence in 11 to 15 year olds by at least 33% by 1994 (from about 8% in 1988 to less than 6%).

1.12   The white paper also set out some specific policy commitments to help achieve these targets in five main areas: price and accessibility; health education and cessation advice; controls on advertising and promotion of non-smoking; and improving scientific understanding.

Progress towards Health of the Nation targets

1.13   The lung cancer mortality rate for men fell by an estimated 13.9% over the four years since the start of the Health of the Nation strategy. Over the same period the mortality rate for women fell by only 2.5%. These data should be interpreted with caution because of the latent period for onset of cancer.

1.14   Preliminary figures from the 1996 General Household Survey[1] (GHS) data published in November 1997 show that, for the first time since smoking questions were included in 1972, the prevalence of cigarette smoking has increased for both men and women. Between 1990 and 1994 the percentage of men smoking cigarettes fell from 31% to 28% and that for women fell from 28% to 26%. In 1996, 29% of men and 28% of women smoked cigarettes, which is a return to 1992 figures. The increase was only statistically significant for women aged 25 - 34 (up from 30% in 1994 to 34% in 1996.) In recent years the fall in smoking prevalence among men and women has been levelling out, but it is not known whether the new figures indicate a trend or a short term fluctuation.

1.15   The General Household Survey also demonstrates that smoking prevalence is closely linked with socio-economic status. In the period between 1974 and 1994 smoking prevalence in professional groups fell by a half, but in unskilled manual workers the fall was only a third. This means that, by 1994, unskilled workers were two to three times more likely to smoke than professionals.

1.16   The 1995 Infant Feeding Survey (IFS)[11], which is retrospective (ie seeking information after the pregnancy) and uses postal questionnaires, monitors smoking in pregnancy and showed that the Health of the Nation year 2000 target may have been met ahead of time. The percentage of pregnant smokers who gave up during pregnancy increased from 24% in 1985 to 33% in 1995. Additionally, 47% smoked fewer cigarettes. The IFS shows that people in lower socioeconomic groups were more likely to smoke before pregnancy and less likely to give up smoking during pregnancy than women in higher groups. For example, 45% of women with partners in non-manual occupations gave up smoking during pregnancy compared with 32% of women with partners in manual occupations and 24% of women with no partner.

1.17   The Health Education Authority survey "Trends in Smoking and Pregnancy 1992 - 1997 [12] is prospective and uses a quota sample to interview pregnant women. This survey gives more information of value, highlighting particular areas for concern which are not identified in IFS[11] questionnaires. For example, more than twice as many women with partners in the unemployed and manual groups smoked compared with those with partners in the non manual groups (39% and 15% respectively), and only one in four pregnant women gave up smoking during pregnancy (26% - this falls short of the Health of the Nation target). The percentage of women who recalled advice from a professional was 49% in the HEA study and 85% in the IFS. This discrepancy could be explained by the increasing likelihood of receiving advice as the pregnancy progresses which indicates that women may not be receiving advice until later in the pregnancy. One third of those receiving advice from general practitioners (GPs) and almost one half who received advice from midwives recall being advised to cut down consumption rather than give up smoking.

1.18   Provisional figures for the year to June 1996 show that 81.2 billion cigarettes were released for home consumption. This represents an annual reduction of roughly 3.1% from the 1990 baseline of 98 billion ie a total reduction of just over 17% in five and a half years. This trend, if continued, would fall short of the target of 40% over 10 years. The figures include an estimate of EU imports for the period following the establishment of the European single market on 1 January 1993.

1.19   Headline figures for 1996, released by the Office for National Statistics (ONS)[13] in July 1997, show that the target for smoking prevalence amongst 11 to 15 year olds was not only missed but *the prevalence level actually rose to 13%* In England in 1996, 11% of boys and 15% of girls were regular smokers. The prevalence figure for 11 to 15 year olds was 12% in 1994 and although the increase is not statisically significant it continues the recent upward trend. Very few children are smokers when they start secondary school, but at the time they reach the fifth year, when they are for the most part 15 years old, about three out of every ten smoke at least one cigarette a week. For 1996 the percentages for male regular smokers at ages 11, 12, 13, 14, and 15 were 1, 2, 8, 13 and 28. For females the percentages for the same ages were: 0, 4, 11, 24 and 33.[12]

Wales - Targets and Progress

1.20   The Strategic Intent and Direction for the NHS in Wales[14] set a target to reduce the mortality rate from lung cancer in those aged 45 - 64 by at least 15% by the year 2002, from a baseline of 124 per 100,000 in men and 44 per 100,000 in women in 1985. Health for All in Wales[15] set the following targets for smoking:

■   to reduce the proportion of men aged 18-64 who smoke daily to 20%, and of women to 17%, by the year 2000, from 35% in men and 30% in women in 1985.

■   to reduce the proportion of 15 year old boys who smoke at least weekly to 11%, and of girls to 14%, by the year 2000, from 15% in boys and 20% in girls in 1986.

1.21   The mortality rate from lung cancer for men aged 45 - 64 fell steadily by approximately one third between 1985 and 1995. There had been about a 10% reduction for women, but little change from 1992 onwards. Health Promotion Wales surveys[16] showed that by 1996 daily smoking amongst men aged 18 - 64 had fallen to 28%, and amongst women to 26%. For 15 year olds, however, the proportion of boys smoking at least weekly had risen to 23%, and girls to 29%.

1.22   In 1997, new health gain targets were announced in Wales, under the New Strategic Plans initiative.[17] These are:

- to reduce European standardised mortality rate for lung cancer in men under the age of 75 by at least 54% by 2010 (from 49.2 per 100,000 in 1995 to no more than 22.6 in 2010).

- to reduce European standardised mortality rate for lung cancer in women under the age of 75 by at least 21% by 2010 (from 23.0 per 100,000 in 1995 to no more than 18.2 in 2010).

- to reduce the proportion of adults age 18 to 64 who smoke (daily and occasionally) to no more than 20% for both men and women by 2002 (from 31.5% in men and 28.1% in women in 1993).

- to reduce the proportion of 15 year old children who smoke (at least weekly) to no more than 16% for boys and 20% for girls (from 23% in boys and 29% in girls in 1996).

- to increase the proportion of women who give up smoking during their pregnancy to at least 33%.

Scotland - Targets and Progress

1.23   In 1992 the policy statement "Scotland's Health: A Challenge to us all"[18] reaffirmed the national targets in relation to smoking set the previous year in "Health Education in Scotland: A National Policy Statement".[19] These targets were to achieve a 30% reduction in the prevalence of smoking in those aged 12-24 years (from 30% to 21%) and a 20% reduction in those aged 25-65 years (from 40% to 32%) between 1986 and 2000.

1.24   In the 1995 Scottish Health Survey[20] interviews were conducted on a random sample of 7932 persons aged 16-64 years. Overall 34% of men and 36% of women were self-reported current smokers. Serum cotinine analysis suggested a degree of under-reporting, giving an adjusted estimate of 43% of men and 38% of women. The prevalence of self-reported smoking in 25-65 year olds was 35% and in 16-24 year olds was 34%.

1.25   The survey showed an association between social class and smoking; 23% of men and 22% of women in Social Classes I and II were self-reported smokers, compared with 49% in respect of both sexes in social classes IV and V.

1.26   The ONS biennial survey of smoking among secondary school children in Scotland[21] has shown no significant improvement in smoking levels in 12-15 year olds between 1982 and 1996. In 1996 22% of boys and 23% of girls in this age group were regular or occasional smokers.

Northern Ireland - Targets and Progress

1.27 The Regional Strategy for the Northern Ireland Health and Personal Social Services 1992-1997[22] set targets to increase the proportion of the population aged 12-64 who do not smoke cigarettes from 70% to 75% and to increase the proportion of children who have not started to smoke. In 1994 a specific target to increase the percentage of 15 year olds who do not smoke to 80% by 1997 was added.

1.28 The Continuous Household Survey 1994/95[23] showed that the proportion of the population who do not smoke cigarettes had increased to 72%. The 1994 Heath Behaviour of School Children in Northern Ireland Survey[24] found that 17% of 11-15 year olds were smokers, 13% of whom smoked at least once weekly. By fifth form 26% of girls and 22% of boys were smoking at least once weekly. Comparison with results of surveys since 1983 show that there has been little change in the proportion of children who smoke.

1.29 The New Northern Ireland Strategy "Regional Strategy for Health and Social Wellbeing 1997-2002"[25] has set new targets for smoking. These are:

■ By 2002 the proportion of the adult population aged 16+ who do not smoke cigarettes should have increased from 72% to 74%.

■ By 2002 the proportion of the population aged 11-15 years who do not smoke cigarettes should have increased from 83% to 85%.

Nicotine Addiction

1.30 Over the past decade there has been increasing recognition that underlying smoking behaviour and its remarkable intractability to change is addiction to the drug nicotine.[26,27] Nicotine has been shown to have effects on brain dopamine systems similar to those of drugs such as heroin and cocaine,[28] and with appropriate reward schedules it functions as a robust reinforcer in animals.[29] Dependence on nicotine is established early in teenagers' smoking careers,[30] and there is compelling evidence that much adult smoking behaviour is motivated by a need to maintain a preferred level of nicotine intake, leading to the phenomenon of nicotine titration, or compensatory smoking in response to lowered nicotine yields.[31] People seeking treatment for heroin, cocaine, or alcohol dependence rate cigarettes as hard to give up as their problem drug.[32] The aversiveness of nicotine withdrawal is an important factor underlying the failure of many attempts at cessation.

Smoking Related Diseases

1.31 A large number of fatal and life-threatening diseases are caused largely or entirely by smoking. They include chronic obstructive pulmonary disease, vascular diseases at various critical sites and several forms of cancer.

1.32 Chronic Obstructive Pulmonary Disease (COPD) is caused by irreversible and usually progressive limitation of airflow and occurs most usually in the form of chronic bronchitis and emphysema. It is a major cause of disability and premature death. The American Cancer Society (CPS II)[33] Study found that cigarette smokers had ten times the risk of dying from COPD than non-smokers; about three-quarters of deaths from this disease were attributable to smoking. In the prospective study of male British doctors[6] cigarette smokers had 13 times the risk of dying of the disease compared to non-smokers and again about three quarters of deaths from this disease were attributable to smoking. The results from these two major prospective studies are remarkably consistent. The importance of smoking as a cause of chronic obstructive pulmonary disease is often overlooked yet it contributes a major burden of disease due to smoking.

1.33 The extent of arterial damage induced by smoking is great. Examples of serious arterial diseases related to smoking include coronary artery disease and heart attacks, aortic aneurysms which can lead to sudden death,[34] carotid artery disease which can lead to strokes[35] and peripheral vascular disease which, in the lower limbs, can lead to severe pain in the leg on walking and may necessitate amputation. [36] Recent data show that smoking causes more rapid expansion of aortic aneurysm.[37]

1.34 Smoking causes increased risk of cancers in several sites, pre-eminently the lung, but also several others such as the oral cavity, pharynx, larynx, oesophagus, pancreas and bladder. The association between smoking and certain cancers of the head and neck is discussed in Part Six.

1.35 The following tables, reproduced with permission from the British Medical Bulletin,[9] give data on fatal diseases positively associated with smoking from the study of male British doctors and the large American Cancer Society study.

Table 1* Fatal diseases positively associated with smoking – study of male British doctors[6]

Disease	STANDARDISED MORTALITY PER 100,000 MEN/YEAR		Relative risk (b/a)	Absolute excess Risk per 100,000 men/year (b-a)	Attributable proportion †(%)
	Life-long non-smoker (a)	Current cigarette smoker (b)			
(i) increased risk largely or entirely caused by smoking					
Cancer of:					
Lung	14	209	15.0	195	31
Upper respiratory sites	1	24	24.0	23	37
Bladder	13	30	2.3	17	28
Pancreas	16	35	2.2	19	26
Ischaemic heart disease	572	392	1.6	320	15
Respiratory heart disease	0	10	–	10	100
Aortic aneurysm	15	62	4.1	47	48
Chronic obstructive lung disease	10	127	12.7	117	78
(ii) increased risk partly caused by smoking					
Cancer of:					
Oesophagus	4	30	7.5	26	56
Stomach	2.6	43	1.7	17	17
Kidney	9	13	2.1	4	25
Leukaemia	4	7	1.3	3	19
Stroke	152	203	1.3	51	3
Pneumonia	71	138	1.9	67	21
(iii) increased risk due to confounding					
Cirrhosis of liver	6	32	5.3	26	–
Cancer of liver	7	11	1.5	4	–
Suicide	23	37	1.5	14	–
Poisoning	7	19	2.7	12	–
All diseases excluding those in category (iii)	907	1323	2.0	916	23
All diseases excluding those in categories (ii) & (iii)	512	1324	2.2	712	26

Results taken from reference 6

† The proportion of all deaths from the specified disease attributable to smoking, assuming 30% of the population are current smokers and that all the excess risk in smokers is due to smoking. In Group (ii) the actual proportions will be somewhat less than those specified.

* Reproduced with the kind permission of the British Council.

Table 2* Fatal diseases positively associated with smoking – American Cancer Society (CPSII). Men and Women aged 35 years or more

Disease		Life-long non-smoker	Current cigarette smoker	Relative risk	Absolute excess Risk per 100,000 per year	Attributable proportion[†] (%)
		STANDARDISED MORTALITY PER 100,000/YEAR[#]				
(i) increased risk largely or entirely caused by smoking						
Cancer of:						
Lung	M	24	537	22.4	513	87
	F	18	213	11.9	195	77
Upper respiratory sites	M	1	27	24.5	26	89
	F	2	10	5.6	8	58
Bladder and other urinary organs	M	18	53	2.9	35	36
	F	8	21	2.6	13	32
Pancreas	M	18	38	2.1	20	25
	F	16	37	2.3	21	29
Ischaemic heart disease	M	500	970	1.9	470	22
	F	386	688	1.8	302	19
Aortic aneurysm [‡]	M	24	98	4.1	74	48
	F	11	52	4.6	41	52
Chronic obstructive pulmonary disease	M	39	378	9.7	339	72
	F	21	216	10.5	195	74
(ii) increased risk partly caused by smoking						
Cancer of:						
Oesophagus	M	9	68	7.6	59	66
	F	4	41	10.3	37	74
Kidney	M	8	23	3.0	15	37
	F	6	8	1.4	2	11
Cerebrovascular lesions	M	147	328	2.2	181	27
	F	236	434	1.8	198	20
(iii) increased risk due to confounding						
Cancer of cervix	F	8	18	2.1	10	–
All diseases excluding those in category (iii)	M	788	2520	3.2	1732	40
	F	708	1720	2.4	1012	30
All diseases excluding those in categories (ii) & (iii)	M	588	2010	3.4	1422	42
	F	438	1179	2.7	741	34

Relative risks taken from the American Cancer Study (CPSII) [33]

[#] Calculated using the published relative risk, the mortality in the population aged> 35 years [9] and asuming that 30% of the population are current smokers

[†] The proportion of all deaths from the specified disease attributable to smoking, assuming 30% of the population are current smokers and that all the excess risk in smokers is due to smoking. In Group (ii) the actual proportions will be somewhat less than those specified.

[‡] Taken from American Cancer Society (CPSII) [33]

* Reproduced with the kind permission of the British Council.

1.36   Smoking in pregnancy causes adverse outcomes notably miscarriage, reduced birth weight for gestation and perinatal death. Where parents continue to smoke after pregnancy there is an increased rate of sudden infant death syndrome.

1.37   The list of other diseases known to be associated with smoking includes cataracts, hip fracture (osteoporosis), and periodontal disease.[9]

Conclusions

1.38   Smoking is a major cause of illness and death from chronic respiratory diseases, cardiovascular disease, and cancers of the lung and other sites.

1.39   Smoking is the most important cause of premature death in developed countries. It accounts for one fifth of deaths in the UK: some 120,000 deaths a year.

1.40   The avoidance of smoking would eliminate one third of the cancer deaths in Britain and one sixth of the deaths from other causes.

1.41   Smoking prevalence in young people rose between 1988 and 1997 and the downward trend in adult smoking, noted in the UK since 1972, was reversed in 1996.

1.42   A person who smokes regularly more than doubles his or her risk of dying before the age of 65.

1.43   Addiction to nicotine sustains cigarette smoking and is responsible for the remarkable intractability of smoking behaviour.

1.44   Smoking in pregnancy causes adverse outcomes, notably an increased risk of miscarriage, reduced birth weight and perinatal death. If parents continue to smoke after pregnancy there is an increased rate of sudden infant death syndrome.

1.45   Cigarette smoking is an important contributor to health inequalities, being much more common amongst the disadvantaged than the affluent members of society.

Recommendations

1.46   The enormous damage to health and life arising from smoking should no longer be accepted; the Government should take effective action to limit this preventable epidemic.

1.47   The Government should require of the tobacco industry:

    a.   reasonable standards in the assessment of evidence relating to the health effects of the product it sells,

    b.   acceptance that smoking is a major cause of premature death, and

    c.   normal standards of disclosure of the nature and magnitude of the hazards of smoking to their customers, comparable to that expected from other manufacturers of consumer products.

1.48   Independently of specific governmental regulations, tobacco manufacturers should comply with these requirements.

1.49   There is an importance and urgency with the smoking problem that needs to be recognised by both the Government and the public.

PART TWO

ENVIRONMENTAL TOBACCO SMOKE

Background

2.1 The Third Report[38] of the ISCSH (1983) recorded a tentative link between exposure to environmental tobacco smoke (ETS) and lung cancer. This topic was pursued in more detail in the Fourth Report[39] of the ISCSH (1988) in the light of information published since the Third Report and in response to increasing public concern about the postulated link between ETS and a number of adverse health effects.

2.2 After making allowances for misclassification of smokers and other confounding factors, the Fourth Report[39] of the ISCSH concluded that there was an increase in the risk of lung cancer from exposure to environmental tobacco smoke in the range of 10% to 30%. This meant that people who had never smoked, but who had been exposed to environmental tobacco smoke through most of their lives, had a 10% to 30% higher risk of lung cancer than non-smokers who were not exposed to tobacco smoke. The Fourth Report[39] also concluded that ETS might have other effects on health, and recommended that continued attention should be given to the role of ETS in the occurrence of respiratory illnesses in children.

2.3 In 1992 the United States Environmental Protection Agency published a report entitled "Respiratory Health Effects of Passive Smoking: lung cancer and other disorders".[40] It confirmed the findings published in the Fourth Report[39] on exposure to environmental tobacco smoke and lung cancer risk and also identified additional links between passive smoking and certain childhood illnesses.

2.4 At the inaugural meeting of SCOTH (1994), Committee members decided to undertake a comprehensive review of the health effects of exposure to ETS. It was agreed to update the assessment published in the Fourth Report[39] on the effect of ETS exposure in relation to lung cancer and to respiratory diseases in children, to consider the effect of ETS exposure on the development of ischaemic heart disease, and to examine whether ETS had deleterious effects on fetal growth and preterm delivery.

Environmental Tobacco Smoke and Lung Cancer

2.5 Since earlier assessments by the National Research Council,[41] the US Department of Health and Human Services,[42] the fourth report of the ISCSH,[39] the Australian report of the National Health and Medical Research Council (NHMRC) Working Party,[43] and the US Environmental Protection Agency report (EPA)[40] the number of epidemiological studies of ETS and lung cancer has more than doubled and there are additional data on the effect of biases, dietary confounding and the use of biomarkers to measure exposure to ETS.

2.6   An updated assessment on lung cancer and ETS[44] was commissioned by the Department of Health. This consisted of a review of the relevant literature with a meta-analysis of the epidemiological studies. It was prepared by Mr A Hackshaw, Dr M Law and Professor N Wald and was considered by the Committee in 1997. The results of this review confirmed earlier conclusions that exposure to ETS is a cause of lung cancer.

2.7   The Committee also had sight of the of the California Environmental Protection Agency 1997 report "Health Effects of Exposure to Environmental Tobacco Smoke"[45] and the Commonwealth of Australia NHMRC scientific information paper on "The Health Effects of Passive Smoking", November 1997. [46] Both these reports concluded that passive smoking caused lung cancer.

DH Commissioned Report on ETS and Lung Cancer[44]

2.8   This report, which was based on an analysis of 37 epidemiological studies of lung cancer in women who were life-long non-smokers living with smokers, showed that women had a statistically significant excess risk of lung cancer of 24% (95% confidence intervals, 13 - 36%). The analysis also showed that there was a dose response relationship between the risk of lung cancer and the number of cigarettes smoked by a person's partner, as well as the duration over which they had been exposed to their smoke. After adjusting for potential biases (misclassification and underestimation) and dietary confounding, the authors concluded that the underestimation of risk because of exposure to ETS in the reference group tended to cancel out the effects of misclassification bias and dietary confounding, so that the unadjusted (that is the observed) pooled relative risk from epidemiological studies provided a valid estimate of the true risk of lung cancer due to passive smoking. Overall the authors concluded that the evidence (epidemiological, dosimetric and toxicological) leads to the conclusion that breathing other people's tobacco smoke causes lung cancer in non-smokers. After adjustment for biases and confounding, the estimated excess risk is 26% (95% confidence interval 7-47%) which equates to several hundred deaths per year in Britain. The accumulation of evidence did not alter the earlier scientific assessment, and the present estimate is unlikely to be significantly altered by the accumulation of additional information.

Tobacco Manufacturers' Association submission on ETS and Lung Cancer

2.9   The Committee received from the Tobacco Manufacturers' Association (TMA) a submission of scientific evidence and reference papers which presented an account of the epidemiological evidence on ETS and lung cancer. The papers addressed the issues of confounding variables such as diet, air pollution, life style and also other issues such as misdiagnosis, misclassification bias, recall bias and publication bias. The use of cotinine as a bio-marker, and the epidemiology of weak associations were examined. The TMA report concluded that "When all the results are considered, and even when meta-analysis is used, the epidemiological data do not support an inference of causality or even genuinely elevated risk".

2.10   The TMA also drew attention to a "European Working Group Report": ETS: An evaluation of the risk (April 1995),[47] the Congressional Research Service Report: ETS and lung cancer risk (November 1995)[48] and a paper by Armitage A K et al (1997) entitled "Environmental Tobacco Smoke - is it really a carcinogen?".[45]

2.11 The TMA responded to the publication of the paper by Hackshaw and colleagues[44] by submitting a further commentary to the Committee. SCOTH members considered this supplementary commentary alongside all the other data but did not accept the TMA's position. (See also para. 2.13 below).

Review by the Committee on Carcinogenicity

2.12 The TMA submission was also evaluated separately by the Department of Health's Committee on Carcinogenicity of Chemicals in Food, Consumer Products and the Environment (CoC). The CoC not only assessed the paper by Hackshaw and colleagues[44] and the TMA submission but also considered additional evidence such as the chemical composition of ETS and the presence of genotoxic carcinogens in ETS, exposure to ETS and deposition of genotoxic carcinogens in the respiratory tract. The CoC also considered the mutagenicity data on ETS particulates and the available animal inhalation studies with side stream smoke. Particular attention was paid to the available publications dealing with the investigation of carcinogen-adducts with blood proteins and the excretion of tobacco specific carcinogens in the urine of non-smokers exposed to ETS. Taking all the supporting data into consideration the COC concluded that passive smoking in non-smokers exposed over a substantial part of their life is associated with a 10-30% increase in the risk of lung cancer. The detailed conclusions of the CoC are attached at **Annex H.**

2.13 The CoC also considered the supplementary TMA commentary and concluded that there are no new data in the TMA commentary to change the conclusion of the Committee.

Report of a "European Working Group" on ETS and Lung Cancer[46]

2.14 The "European Working Group", which was supported by the tobacco industry, concluded that there is no elevated risk of lung cancer from ETS exposure. The Group decided that, although meta-analysis showed a weak association of lung cancer risk with having a husband who smokes and some indication of a dose-response, this could be explained by misclassification and confounding. SCOTH members noted that the report had not been independently peer reviewed. There was no narrative account of the methods used and only a brief description of the meta-analysis. The report omitted relevant published genotoxicity and adduct studies. The inclusion criteria for studies were not adequately explained. It was thought that the division of the data into small subsets was inappropriate. The failure to investigate and take account of heterogeneity was noted. The omission of results on male never smokers, and failure to consider the increase in lung cancer risk associated with underestimation bias while allowing for the reduction in the risk due to misclassification bias was also noted. The Committee agreed that this report was an unsatisfactory examination of the scientific position and led to incorrect conclusions.

2.15 The "European Working Group" Report was assessed in 1996 in an article by Davey Smith and Phillips[50] which also considered the Philip Morris media campaign (see para. 2.31 below). The authors concluded that, "...the partial and biased nature [of the advertisements] and "expert" report at the heart of the latest industry campaign represents a continuation of its characteristic behaviour". The article drew attention to a report from the industry to the US Tobacco Institute as long ago as 1978 which stated that public worries about smoking were "the most dangerous development to the long term viability of the tobacco industry that has yet occurred" and that "the strategic and long run antidote to the passive smoking issue is...developing and widely publicising clear-cut, credible medical evidence that passive smoking is not harmful to the non-smoker's health". Twenty years on the Committee has not seen such evidence.

Report of the United States Congressional Research Service[48]

2.16   The Congressional Research Service (CRS) provides a service to Congress and is funded by the US Government. The CRS report was not peer reviewed and the authors themselves comment that it was produced under resource constraints which precluded detailed review of all relevant studies. Committee members noted that the Report gave undue prominence to studies from within the industry or from its consultants. Problems connected with misclassification of smokers and the question of threshold effects were presented as seriously threatening the conclusion that ETS causes lung cancer, but much of the discussion was hypothetical and speculative. Members agreed that the Report did not critically challenge the detailed reviews by independent scientists, concluding that ETS causes lung cancer in non smokers.

Summary and Conclusions from SCOTH's Review of ETS and Lung Cancer

2.17   Members reviewed all the evidence on ETS and lung cancer discussed in the preceding paragraphs. They noted the extensive review provided by the CoC and accepted that Committee's overall conclusions: in particular it was noted that exposure to ETS leads to the delivery of genotoxic carcinogens to all parts of the respiratory tract. Reservations were expressed over the methodology of the TMA submission: it contained only a limited narrative and appropriate sensitivity analyses were not undertaken. Members noted that the results obtained for smoking by husband or by spouse were consistent with the findings of the US Environmental Protection Agency in 1992.[40] Geographical heterogeneity had been introduced by a paper from China which yielded a relative risk of 0.79 which, if real, would indicate a protective effect of passive smoking. Although adjustment was made for confounding by misclassification bias, no adjustment was made for other potential sources of confounding, such as underestimation bias. No meta-analysis of dose response was undertaken although individual studies of limited statistical power were assessed for dose response. The Committee concluded that the TMA submission failed to examine the available evidence as a whole, notably that inhaling tobacco smoke from active smoking was a potent cause of lung cancer, (the TMA declined to express an opinion on this issue when asked by the Committee); that genotoxic carcinogens present in ETS were inhaled and absorbed by non-smokers and that the level of risk of lung cancer due to ETS exposure was consistent with the expected risk estimated from the effect of active smoking taking into account the lower exposure. The TMA did not give reasons why, in the light of this evidence, they reached their negative conclusion.

2.18   Members accepted the methods of analysis used by Mr Hackshaw and colleagues. The paper included a narrative review. Exclusion of one particular study (the one from China referred to above) removed any evidence of heterogeneity. Members accepted the exclusion of this study which gave implausible results and also noted the authors' own comment that the effect of ETS could have been obscured by another cause of lung cancer: exposure to open coal fires with little ventilation. Appropriate adjustments were made for misclassification bias by current and former smokers and for dietary confounding. A meta-analysis of dose responses was undertaken. A sensitivity analysis was carried out for misclassification which supported the risk estimation. SCOTH members noted that both submitted meta-analytical reports (i.e. that of the TMA and that of Mr Hackshaw and colleagues) gave similar risk estimates to that of the EPA,[40] but differing conclusions had been drawn on the relevance of confounding and biases. The conclusions of the paper prepared by Mr Hackshaw and colleagues were judged to have been based on the totality of the evidence and an appropriate consideration of the epidemiological data in the context of other available evidence, including that from active smoking.

2.19   SCOTH members concluded that long term exposure of non-smokers to ETS caused an increased risk of lung cancer which, in those living with smokers, is in the region of 20-30%.

2.20   In the Fourth Report of the ISCSH[39] it was thought helpful to explain exactly what the increased risk meant. For clarity that explanation is repeated here: If the risk of lung cancer in non-exposed non-smokers is 10 per 100,000, based on rates in non-smokers in the 35+ age group,[51] a 20-30% increased risk in exposed non-smokers would be a rate of 12-13 per 100,000 per year. Thus we would expect an additional 2-3 lung cancer cases a year per 100,000 non-smokers regularly exposed to ETS. The numbers of people so exposed are not known precisely but an estimate would suggest about several hundred extra lung cancer deaths a year are caused by exposure to passive smoking.[44] There are about 35,000 lung cancer deaths in the United Kingdom per year: it is estimated that 30,000 of these are directly attributable to active smoking.

Environmental Tobacco Smoke and Respiratory Diseases in Children

2.21   The U.S. Surgeon General's 1986 report[42] and that of the Environmental Protection Agency (1992)[40] considered the evidence associating parental smoking and respiratory diseases in childhood. A systematic review of research studies from which, where possible, summary estimates of the relative risks or odds ratios were produced, was carried out for the Department of Health by Dr Derek Cook, Professor Ross Anderson and Professor David Strachan.[52] An Executive Summary of this review is to be found at **Annex I.** The authors were particularly concerned to consider the importance of residual confounding from other environmental factors, to assess the importance of exposure at different ages, and to distinguish between pre- and post-natal exposure. The following topics were considered: sudden infant death; lower respiratory tract illness in preschool children; prevalence of asthma and respiratory symptoms in schoolchildren; incidence, severity and prognosis of asthma; bronchial reactivity; allergic sensitisation and ear disease and adenotonsillectomy.

2.22   The authors reviewed the evidence on parental smoking and sudden infant death syndrome (SIDS) and acute lower respiratory illness (LRI) in infancy and concluded that the relationship was causal. The elevated risks associated with smoking by other household members indicated that post-natal exposure was the predominant cause. For SIDS the adjusted pooled odds ratio for maternal smoking was 2.08 (95% CI, 1.90-2.21) ie. a doubling of risk. For LRI in infancy the pooled odds ratio for either parent smoking was 1.48 (95% CI, 1.40-1.57) and for maternal smoking was 1.64 (95% CI, 1.54-1.73). The associations with lower respiratory illness remained after adjustment for confounding factors and showed evidence of dose response.

2.23   There was also convincing evidence that parental smoking increased the risk of asthma and respiratory symptoms in schoolchildren, although at a lower risk than for infants. Maternal smoking had a greater effect than paternal smoking. There was evidence of a dose response relationship between risk and the number of smokers in the home for all symptoms (asthma, wheeze, cough, phlegm and breathlessness). The pooled odds ratios, where children were exposed to two parents smoking, were 1.52 (95% CI, 1.34-1.72) for asthma, 1.40 (95% CI, 1.29-1.51) for wheeze and 1.61 (95% CI, 1.50-1.73) for cough.

2.24   The report on bronchial hyper-reactivity summarised effect measures from eight studies with a pooled estimate of relative odds of 1.28 (95% CI, 1.08-1.52). Six other investigations did not show statistically significant effects and results from a further four studies were unpublished. It was concluded that the relationship between bronchial hyperactivity and ETS could have been overestimated by positive publication bias. No consistent association was found between parental smoking and allergic sensitisation. Significant and unexplained heterogeneity of odds ratios between studies created difficulties for interpretation. It was concluded that ETS exposure was not consistently related to allergic sensitisation and the relationship with bronchial hyper-reactivity had not been established.

2.25   It was also concluded that parental smoking caused acute and chronic middle ear disease in children, the pooled odds ratios for recurrent otitis media if either parent smoked being 1.41 (1.19-1.65), and for middle ear effusion, 1.38 (1.23-1.55).

Environmental Tobacco Smoke and Ischaemic Heart Disease

2.26   Meta-analyses of the epidemiological studies indicated a relative risk of ischaemic heart disease (IHD) of about 1.3 (an excess risk of 30%) in non-smokers exposed to environmental tobacco smoke compared to those not exposed. This effect appears implausibly large, since the relative risk of IHD with active smoking is about two-fold and exposure, based on urinary cotinine studies, is only equivalent to about 1% of that from actively smoking. With a linear dose-response relationship the expected relative risk would be 1.01 (1% of the excess risk of about 100% from active smoking). An explanation for this substantial difference was needed.

2.27   The evidence on active and passive smoking and IHD was reviewed in a paper prepared for the Committee[53] by Dr Malcolm Law, Dr J Morris and Professor Nicholas Wald which suggested an explanation. Part of the association was due to dietary difference between non-smokers who live with smokers and those who do not, and part of the association was judged to be causal. The best estimate of the reversible (cause and effect) component of the association is a relative risk of 1.23 or an excess risk of 23% in non-smokers exposed to ETS compared to those not exposed. The main causal factor appears to be an increase in platelet aggregation, a major step in the formation of thrombi, which may occlude the coronary arteries. The dose-response relationship between ETS exposure and platelet aggregation is non-linear and is consistant with results from other studies of the effects of tobacco smoke on platelet aggregation. The Committee concluded that there was a cause and effect relationship between passive smoking and IHD and that enhanced platelet aggregation was a plausible mechanism. It was also noted that there were other possible mechanisms by which ETS exposure could have an adverse effect on the cardiovascular system, including reduction in oxygen transportation to the heart, acceleration of atherosclerosis[53] and increases in plasma fibrinogen. If the size of the effect was as great as Law et al estimated, it would represent a significant public health problem. The Committee, in drawing their conclusions, considered a commentary on the Law et al paper[44] which was received from the TMA.

2.28   The Committee noted the US prospective study of passive smoking among 32,000 nurses which reported an increased IHD risk, judged to be largely causal. (Kawachi et al.)[54]

Environmental Tobacco Smoke and Pregnancy Outcome

2.29   The Committee noted the Avon Longitudinal Survey of Pregnancy and Childbirth (ALSPAC) which is a prospective study and includes 14,100 live births. They were grateful to receive a report[55] by Professor Jean Golding on preliminary analyses related to "Passive Smoking and Outcome of Pregnancy".

The Confidential Enquiry into Stillbirths and Deaths in Infancy

2.30   The Committee considered the Report of the National Advisory Board of the Confidential Enquiry into Stillbirths and Deaths in Infancy (CESDI)[56] and the subsequent publication in the British Medical Journal in July 1996.[57] This case - control study shows that after controlling for maternal smoking during pregnancy, ETS was significantly associated with the sudden infant death syndrome. The adjusted odds ratio for paternal smoking was 2.50 and if both parents smoked, 3.79. There was a dose-response effect. These odds ratios are consistent with previously published studies. This study was included in the commissioned systematic review.[48]

Philip Morris "Passive Smoking Campaign"

2.31   In June 1996, Philip Morris launched an advertisment campaign in newspapers in a number of European countries. The aim of the campaign was to undermine public health messages about the health risks of passive smoking. The Committee were aware that the Advertising Standards Authority (ASA) received complaints about the Philip Morris campaign which compared the risk of passive smoking with a variety of other everyday activities like eating a biscuit, eating pepper frequently, drinking milk or chlorinated water and cooking frequently with rapeseed oil. The complaint that the advertisements misrepresented the findings of the studies (quoted in the advertisments) was upheld and, in a report published in October 1996, the Authority said "...it considered that the advertisement gave the misleading impression that passive smoking had been conclusively proved to pose less danger to the health of UK consumers than the five activities placed above it in the table in the advertisement. The Authority asked the advertisers to withdraw the advertisement".

Conclusions

2.32   Exposure to environmental tobacco smoke is a cause of lung cancer and, in those with long term exposure, the increased risk is in the order of 20-30%.

2.33   Exposure to environmental tobacco smoke is a cause of ischaemic heart diseases and if current published estimates of magnitude of relative risk are validated, such exposure represents a substantial public health hazard.

2.34   Smoking in the presence of infants and children is a cause of serious respiratory illness and asthmatic attacks.

2.35   Sudden infant death syndrome, the main cause of post-neonatal death in the first year of life, is associated with exposure to environmental tobacco smoke. The association is judged to be one of cause and effect.

2.36 Middle ear disease in children is linked with parental smoking and this association is likely to be causal.

Recommendations

2.37 Smoking in public places should be restricted on the grounds of public health. The level of restriction should vary according to the different categories of public place but smoking should not be allowed in public service buildings or on public transport, other than in specially designated and isolated areas. Wherever possible, smoking should not be allowed in the work place.

2.38 There is a need for public education about the risks of smoking in the home particularly in relation to respiratory diseases in children.

2.39 Health education programmes should focus on the dangers of ETS in fetal development and, postnatally, in the sudden infant death syndrome.

PART THREE

THE INFLUENCE OF PRICE AND PROMOTION ON TOBACCO CONSUMPTION

3.1   The Committee focused on the influence of price and promotion (in all its manifestations) on young people because of their vulnerability and susceptiblity to adult influences. It is also known that almost all smokers start to smoke as children or young adults. There is concern to limit consumption and encourage cessation in adults as well as the young and there is evidence that price and promotion influence consumption among existing smokers.[58]

3.2   The dilemma that tobacco consumption has fallen least amongst the poorest families and the regressive effect this has on dependent children, has been discussed by Marsh and MacKay in their book "Poor Smokers".[59] Tobacco tax recovers for the Treasury 17% of the means tested benefits paid to poor smokers by the DSS (1991 figures).

3.3   The subject of price and consumption of tobacco was addressed in the British Medical Bulletin by Joy Townsend.[9] She pointed out that, before the widespread publicity about the health effects of smoking in the early 1960s, there was little difference between the smoking habits of different socio-economic groups. Price has a major effect on cigarette consumption and thus on smoking related diseases, especially in low income groups. It is one of the most powerful elements in strategies for the control of tobacco and is recommended by WHO and other authoritative bodies.[9] Cigarette consumption decreases by about 0.5% for a 1% increase in price adjusted for inflation; the effect is greater in low income groups[9] which may be the groups least susceptible to health education messages.

3.4   Tobacco promotion helps to recruit young smokers, and this promotion occurs without manufacturers making clear the true extent of the harm the products cause and the risk of addiction.

3.5   The Committe received a detailed overview of the marketing challenges facing the UK tobacco industry from Mr Peter Haynes, Marketing Manager of Wellcome. He explained that the marketing objectives of the industry are to encourage smokers to consume more, to undermine motivation to quit, to encourage former smokers to begin again, to encourage adults to start smoking and to hope that the young will experiment and therefore become the pool of new customers. It has been suggested that the industry needs to recruit more than 300 new smokers a day to replace those who die from smoking related diseases.

3.6   The industry approaches the challenge of retention and recruitment of smokers by spending an estimated £60 - 100 million (1994) on promotion. This is described as brand strengthening. It funds a body (Freedom Organisation for the Right to Enjoy Smoking Tobacco - FOREST) to counter the anti-smoking lobbies (retention) and promotes the generic message that smoking is socially acceptable. Generic promotion is subtle and carried out by role models such as fashion models, film and pop stars and television personalities. For example, it is reported that a film star accepted $500,000 from a tobacco company in 1993 to promote its brand in five feature films including Rambo. (The Times - 13.9.94). It is not possible that such promotion would have a favourable influence on brand choice without encouraging the smoking habit.

3.7 Sports sponsorship serves two purposes - firstly promotion of the brand and secondly by subverting the argument that smoking is a health risk (by association with healthy sports role models).

3.8 Even packaging conveys a product of high quality and therefore the inference that the contents are not harmful despite the health warning.

Conclusions

3.9 Price, advertising and promotion influence cigarette consumption.

3.10 Prevalence of smoking in the UK is increasingly associated with factors of social and economic deprivation.

Recommendations

3.11 The real price of tobacco products should continue to be increased each year to reduce consumption

3.12 All forms of tobacco advertising, promotion and identifiable sponsorship should be banned.

PART FOUR

SMOKING AND YOUNG PEOPLE_____

Introduction

4.1   One meeting was devoted to the topic of smoking and young people. The purpose was to review understanding of the factors influencing young people to smoke and to inform wider thinking on this issue. The Committee noted the importance of stopping young people from experimenting with smoking, given the intensely addictive properties of nicotine.

The Health of the Nation

4.2   The Health of the Nation White Paper[10] recognised the importance of reducing the prevalence of smoking in young people. The White Paper included a specific target to reduce the proportion of 11 to 15 year olds who are regular smokers (defined as smoking at least one cigarette a week) from about 8% in 1988 to less than 6% in 1994. Disappointingly, the 1994 target was not met (see para. 1.19). The prevalence of smoking in this group has risen to 13%, and failure to make any impact here contrasts with the continued steady progress in reducing adult smoking prevalence and tobacco consumption.

Australian Experience

4.3   The Australian Quit Evaluation Studies number 8, 1994-1995[56] concluded that smoking among young people is not declining and there are worrying signs that smoking is re-emerging as a signifier of the rejection of authority. Research into the attitudes of young smokers to quitting revealed two strong themes: young people do not believe that smoking is currently doing them any harm and young smokers intend to quit eventually but put off the decision.

A Smoking Target for Young People

4.4   There may be an advantage in reducing the age range of any future targets among young people by focusing on discrete age groups. It is known that nearly all 10 to 11 year olds do not smoke, but by age 15 years about 30% have become smokers. The main change in attitude and behaviour occurs around age 13, with some variation between the sexes. A clearer focus on prevalence in 14 and 15 year olds (Years 10 and 11 of the National Curriculum) might offer a more precise indicator of the success of efforts to reduce smoking in young people. It will be useful to continue to document prevalence changes in smoking in younger age groups in order to provide early warning of any significant changes which might occur. Members considered that, in the future, gender related smoking prevalence for young people should be monitored for age groups 11, 12 - 13 and 14 - 15.

4.5   While the prevalence of regular smoking is an important indicator, information on the proportion of young people who used to smoke but have given up, those who have tried smoking without taking it up regularly and those who have never smoked is also relevant. Useful data are provided in an Exeter Schools Health Education Unit Publication "Young People in 1996".[57] This book, published in July 1997, reported that a quarter of 14 - 15 year old boys and almost a third of the girls, smoked at least one cigarette during the previous week. 20% of the 14 - 15 year olds were able to buy cigarettes from a shop. Within the 14 - 15 year age range, of girls and boys who consider themselves "regular "smokers, only about 6% say that they do *not* want to give up.

Children's Smoking, Taxes and Tobacco Industry Income

4.6   1994 OPCS figures[62] on tax and industry revenue from children's (illegal ie under 16 years of age) smoking were illuminating. In England the total tobacco tax revenue to Treasury from young people was just under £104m (the industry received nearly £29m). Treasury revenue from under age smoking in Scotland was nearly £11 million, in Wales it was over £5 million and in Northern Ireland treasury income was over £4.5 million. Except in Scotland, under aged girls contributed more to treasury revenue than under aged boys. In England and Wales in 1996 there were 140 prosecutions for tobacco sales to minors, with findings of guilt in 119.[63]

Factors Influencing Young People to Smoke

Parents and siblings

4.7   An OPCS enquiry,[64] commissioned by the Department of Health, showed that young people whose parents smoke are twice as likely to smoke as children of non-smoking parents. It also showed that young people who perceive no parental disapproval are seven times more likely to smoke than young people who perceive strong parental disapproval; that young people with a sibling who smokes are up to four times more likely to be regular smokers than those whose siblings do not smoke; and that the effect of peer smoking is more pronounced with increasing age.   A Royal College of Physicians working party report showed that the prevalence of smoking among young people is higher in those living with a single parent and is higher still if the lone parent is a smoker.[65] It should be said that little is known about the relative contribution of family influences and hereditary factors to susceptibility to smoking.

Young People and Price

4.8   It is clear that price plays a definite role in cigarette consumption.   Smoking trends in 15 year olds mirror price changes, indicating that they are responsive to price.[66]

Young People and Nicotine Addiction

4.9   Studies of teenagers have shown that pharmacological motives become important very early in the smoking career. By the time daily smoking is established, within only a few months of starting, children take in as much nicotine per cigarette as do dependent adult smokers.[67]   Children as young as age 14-15 report experiencing nicotine withdrawal effects, and perceive that stopping smoking will be hard to achieve successfully.[68] These observations confirm the US Food and Drug Administration's view of cigarette smoking as a "paediatric disease".[69]

Young People and Cigarette Advertising

4.10   The Committee received evidence from Mr P Haynes, (see para. 3.5), suggesting that key advertising messages exploit the emerging independence of young people. Cigarettes are used as a fashion accessory and appeal to young women. Other influences on young people include the linking of sporting heroes and smoking through sports sponsorship, the use of cigarettes by popular characters in television programmes and cigarette promotions. Research suggests that young people are aware of the most heavily advertised cigarette brands.[70] Mr Haynes suggested that the key objective of the advertisers is to expand the market, using various strategies to persuade young people to smoke more.

4.11   Sports sponsorship is acknowledged by the tobacco industry to be valuable advertising. A Tobacco Industry journal in 1994 described the Formula One car as "The most powerful advertising space in the world".[71] In a letter to the Lancet of 15th November 1997, Professor Anne Charlton and colleagues have described a cohort study carried out in 22 secondary schools in England in 1994 and 1995. Boys whose favourite television sport was motor racing had a 12.8% risk of becoming regular smokers compared to 7.0% of boys who did not follow motor racing. The Committee was concerned at the link between the onset of regular smoking in boys and their preference for watching motor racing sponsored by specific brands of cigarettes.

4.12   The Department of Health's Smee Report 1992[72] examined the effect of year-to-year variations in advertising expenditure within countries and concluded that advertising influenced tobacco consumption. The Smee report also reviewed the effect of advertising bans in other countries. Norway and Finland have complete bans on advertising which were estimated to have reduced cigarette consumption by 9% and 7% respectively. Bans in Canada, Australia and New Zealand resulted in reductions less than in Norway and Finland.

4.13   Although other factors may have been involved, the advertising ban in Norway in 1975 appears to have led to a substantial reduction in smoking among school students and adult males.[69] Between 1973 - 1994 female smoking prevalence in the age group 16 - 24 years fell from about 44% to about 28%. For males of the same age group it fell from more than 45% to 30%. Since 1975, when the advertising ban was introduced in Norway prevalence among male daily smokers aged 13 - 15 fell from 15% to 9% in 1990. For girls the fall was from 17% to just below 10%.[74] The ultimate effect of an advertising ban depends to a certain extent on prior restrictions on smoking.

4.14   The committee noted that a paper published in the Journal of the American Medical Association[75] in 1994 concluded that: "The tobacco advertising campaigns targeting women, which were launched in 1967, were associated with a major increase in smoking uptake that was specific to females younger than the legal age for purchasing cigarettes".

4.15   The long term effect of banning advertising and promotion in Australia and New Zealand, Canada, Norway and Finland and in any other parts of the world instituting a ban, is being watched with interest. Data from New Zealand[76] show that there had not been a decrease in smoking prevalence in those aged 15 years and over between 1991 and 1995. There was a period of marked decline from 1984 to 1990. Among 15-19 year olds smoking prevalence peaked in the first quarter of 1991 and declined in the second half of the year. These changes were thought to be consistent with the heavy tobacco advertising in 1990, the advertising ban from December 1990, and the effect of the 17% cigarette price rise in July 1991. It was concluded in "Tobacco Statistics 1996"[76] that smoking reduced as and when Government intervened, by legislation, taxation, health promotion programmes or publicity campaigns. This document also shows that smoking prevalence amongst Maori people is about double that in Europeans.

4.16   In February 1997, Mrs Christine Godfrey, Health Economist from the University of York, gave a presentation to the Committee on the effects of cigarette advertising on the young. Econometric studies could never provide conclusive evidence of causality ie a direct link between advertising and tobacco consumption. It was therefore necessary to make a judgement on the balance of probabilities, considering all available evidence, not least the marketing intentions and expenditure of tobacco companies.[77]   The dramatic increase in the brand share of the product following the launch of the Joe Camel character in the US demonstrated that marketing activities are directed at placing brands in different sectors of the market. Research has looked at young people's recognition and susceptibility to cigarette advertising or marketing techniques. Susceptible young people go on to become smokers, but it is not clear whether susceptibility pre- or post-dates awareness of advertising.[78]   Media advertising is only part of the industry's wider marketing activities and should not be considered in isolation from sponsorship, competitions and other types of sales promotion.[79]   Evidence from the General Household Survey[1] shows that young people are more likely to smoke heavily promoted brands than older smokers. Current regulations clearly do not protect children from advertising messages. Advertising could also reinforce smoking behaviour, hinder quitting efforts, constrain media coverage of anti-smoking messages and legitimise the smoking habit. The balance of evidence from different types of studies (econometric, experimental and observational), together with examination of the marketing activities of tobacco companies, indicates that advertising influences consumption and that restrictions on advertising and other marketing activities will lead to a reduction in children's smoking.

4.17   The Committee recognised the difficulty in obtaining conclusive evidence on advertising and total tobacco consumption but, having looked at the available evidence, was of the unanimous view that tobaco advertising and promotion influence the uptake of smoking by young people.   Based on firm medical evidence of the health effects of active smoking and exposure to ETS, open advertising and promotion of tobacco products could no longer be justified.

4.18   In March 1997, the American Liggett Group Inc., agreed to a legal settlement with 22 US states. As part of the settlement the company undertakes "to scrupulously avoid any and all advertising that would appeal to children and adolescents". The company will hand over a quarter of its pre-tax profits for the next 25 years to a fund for litigants, and will give warnings on cigarette packs that smoking is addictive. It will be noted that this is the first time that a tobacco company has admitted that cigarette smoking is addictive and causes lung cancer, heart disease and emphysema.

4.19   A proposed settlement with the tobacco industry in America was announced in June, 1997. (The full text of the settlement is available on the internet.[80]) US tobacco companies have agreed to pay $368.5bn (£230bn) over 25 years, in a settlement with the Attorneys General from forty states, in return for limitations on future litigation. The deal proposes that teenage smoking should fall by 30% in five years and 60% in ten years with penalties against the tobacco companies if these targets are not met. The proposals, which have yet to be endorsed by the President and approved by Congress, will also ban billboard advertising, store displays, sports promotion and the use of human and cartoon images.

Recent Department of Health Funded Research about Smoking and Young People

4.20 A study on protective factors in adolescent smoking was carried out for the Department of Health.[81] The authors concluded that certain factors operate as protective influences against smoking and are not necessarily the inverse of risk factors. Parental influence was seen to decrease during adolescence as peer influence increased. The importance of self-image or social identity was central.

4.21 The study recommended that interventions should have a family and community component as well as a school component; clear and consistent messages should be promulgated from trusted sources of similar age and from role models in sports and media. There should be promotion of the non-smoking image, stricter monitoring of illegal tobacco sales and better dissemination of existing information on the health effects of cigarette smoking.

4.22 The Exeter Schools' data[61] show the higher percentages of smoking girls than boys in the older age groups (years 9, 10 and 11). This is confirmed by information form ONS,[13] reporting a statistically significant increase among 15 year old boys from 19% in 1993 to 26% in 1994. Although there was also an increase in smoking among girls of this age, from 26% to 30%, it was not statistically significant. Social representation and social identity are important factors with respect to smoking and young people; social representation defines the special features of a social group and social identity relates to an individual's persistent sense of self and of sharing significant characteristics with others.

4.23 A quantitative/behavioural study on "Why do young girls smoke?" was commissioned by the Department of Health.[78] The authors concluded that young adolescent girls smoked more cigarettes than boys. Living in single parent families or step families was a risk factor compared with living with both parents, as was the presence in the home of smokers. Peer influences were of considerable importance: having a best friend who smoked was identified as a significant risk factor for smoking. Intentions to smoke were predictive of future smoking behaviour six months later. Adolescents were aware of the health risks associated with smoking and of the addictive nature of smoking. Sensation seeking and non conformist aspects of adolescent identity appeared to be important determinants of smoking. The culture of the particular school influenced smoking prevalence over and above social background factors.

4.24 The authors made recommendations for interventions and indicated that school interventions alone were insufficient to deal with the problem of smoking in young people. Other measures necessary to achieve any substantial change included effective non smoking policies in all public institutions, a ban on all forms of tobacco promotion, and fiscal measures to increase the price of tobacco products above inflation and above increases in disposable income. Specific recommendations for health education programmes should have a shifting focus throughout the school curriculum to tie in with the developmental changes in young people as they mature. Adequate training of teachers was necessary and health education should have a more prominent place in the National Curriculum.

Conclusions

4.25   Targeting of young people by tobacco companies is of particular relevance because of the now acknowledged addictive nature of tobacco.

4.26   Price, advertising and promotion influence cigarette consumption among young people.

4.27   Interventions to prevent smoking in young people should form part of concerted action involving all agencies including home, school, community and Government.

Recommendations

4.28   Young people, in particular, should be protected by a ban on all forms of tobacco advertising and promotion.

4.29   The real price of tobacco products should continue to be increased each year to discourage young people from smoking.

4.30   Changes in smoking prevalence in younger age groups should be monitored.

4.31   Educating young people about tobacco addiction and its effects on health should remain an important part of the school curriculum.

4.32   Young people themselves should be involved in looking at constructive ways of reducing initiation of smoking.

PART FIVE

SMOKING CESSATION

Smoking Cessation Interventions

5.1   Many approaches have been developed to help people stop smoking. In order to arrive at a clearer idea of their effectiveness, the Committee received the results of a systematic review of the efficacy of smoking cessation interventions, based on the analysis of data from 188 randomised controlled trials. The review has since been published in the Archives of Internal Medicine.[83] The report concluded that routine advice by family doctors to give up smoking is useful, and that nicotine replacement therapy in nicotine dependent people is effective.

5.2   Other interventions include psychological approaches such as behavioural techniques. Pharmacological treatments currently available in the UK, other than nicotine replacement therapy, are not effective. (See also paras. 5.11 and 9.3)

Guidelines

5.3   The Committee noted a publication by the United States Agency for Health Care Policy and Research (AHCPR) entitled Smoking Cessation Clinical Practice Guideline (1996).[84] The Guideline, which was based on a careful analysis of scientific evidence, concluded that a number of effective interventions to help people stop smoking are available and should be incorporated into the routine practice of medicine. Both brief and more intensive counselling and support are effective and have their place. The Committee noted that the Health Education Authority is developing similar guidelines for the National Health Service.

5.4   The Committee agreed that standardisation of the timing and nature of advice provided by doctors and midwives to pregnant smokers (see para. 1.17) should be promoted and the effectiveness of such measures should be evaluated.

Advice and Encouragement

5.5   The results of the review[83] show that simple, brief, unsolicited advice from a general practitioner (GP) is effective in increasing rates of smoking cessation. An estimated 2% of smokers, given advice by their GP, stopped smoking and did not relapse up to one year as a direct consequence of such advice. The Cochrane Collaboration review confirmed the effectiveness of GP smoking cessation advice.[85] This form of intervention is extremely cost effective.

5.6   Additional interventions, supplementary to simple advice, such as follow up letters and visits, show mixed results.

5.7   The contribution made by health promotion clinics, which are usually run by nurses, is unknown. Two trials have been undertaken but they lacked sufficient statistical power for reliable conclusions to be drawn.

5.8   Advice and encouragement to stop smoking are known to be more effective in some groups at particularly high risk of the adverse effects such as pregnant women, patients who have ischaemic heart disease or who have recently had a heart attack. There is no available evidence on interventions in sufferers from asthma or in others at times of stress, such as prospective fathers or people awaiting elective surgery under general anaesthesia.

Nicotine Replacement Therapy

5.9   Nicotine Replacement Therapy (NRT) approximately doubles the rate of smoking cessation from simple advice from GPs or more intensive clinic interventions.[86] Nicotine 2mg chewing gum and nicotine patch are comparable in efficacy, but the nicotine patch is more convenient. NRT is best viewed as a treatment adjunct rather than as a complete treatment in itself. It will not help smokers who lack motivation to stop.

5.10 There is now compelling evidence that addiction to the drug nicotine lies at the heart of the smoking problem. It has been said that people smoke for the nicotine from cigarettes but die from the tar. Some authorities advocate a harm reduction approach and suggest that nicotine replacement products could be given to heavily dependent smokers on a long term basis to reduce exposure to toxins and reduce morbidity and mortality.[87,88] The justification for this approach is not that nicotine itself is harm free, but that in a pure form it is much less harmful than smoking.[89] There is a persuasive analogy which likens the cigarette to a dirty drug syringe and points to the potential benefits of a clean delivery system (NRT). Since smoking related diseases show clear evidence of dose and duration response, even partial and temporary reductions in total smoke exposure are likely to lower risk. On present evidence, nicotine from currently available pharmaceutical preparations does not pose a major threat to health.[90] Nevertheless, there is an obvious need to study the effects of long term use of NRT by persistent smokers and to establish the relationship between smoking reduction and reduced incidence of disease.

5.11 Convincing support for other forms of pharmacological treatment from randomised controlled trials is lacking, but the Committee noted that the Food and Drug Administration (FDA) of America has approved the anti-depressant bupropion (see **Part Nine**) for smoking cessation (prescription only). The FDA has also approved, on prescription only, a new nicotine "inhaler" device. This delivers nicotine, from a cartridge, for absorption through the buccal mucosa. The device, which was also launched in the UK in January 1998, is the first to provide smokers with the hand-to-mouth ritual associated with smoking.

Increasing the Accessability to NRT Products

5.12 At present, NRT products, other than the nasal spray, are only available in the UK over the counter from pharmacists. Decreasing the cost of nicotine gum appears to increase the amount used, short-term cessation rates and attempts at cessation.[91] Since 1996 NRT has been widely available in the United States and an article in the Centers for Disease Control Morbidity and Mortality Weekly Report (MMWR - 19.9.97) describes the effectiveness of a health education campaign (the Great American Smokeout), sponsored by the American Cancer Society, which included promotion of NRT products. Sales increased by 30% during one week, thought to be to new purchasers. The article concludes that "marketing and promotion efforts designed to promote attempts to quit, along with OTC (over the counter) availability of nicotine medications, are a useful part of a national strategy to decrease the prevalence of smoking". It should be noted that the OTC category in the US is equivalent to the General Sales List in the United Kingdom. Before FDA approval was granted for OTC sales of NRT, extensive studies were performed on the safety and efficacy of these products when obtained by members of the public without health professional supervision. A paper which estimates the impact of allowing sales of nicotine medications in the US on increasing the number of smokers quitting is to be published in Tobacco Control.[92]

NRT and Pregnancy

5.13   Because the adverse effects of smoking in pregnancy are well known, many women stop smoking before or during pregnancy and active programmes to encourage and assist smoking cessation can achieve further cessation. Unfortunately some of the heaviest smokers continue to smoke. Nicotine replacement therapy has not been evaluated in pregnancy because nicotine probably contributes to the deficit in birthweight in the babies of cigarette smokers.[93] However a review of the pharmacology of cigarette smoking and NRT has concluded that NRT results in lower plasma cotinine levels than heavy cigarette smoking, except during sleep.[94] The American Agency for Health Care Policy and Research (AHCPR)[84] has suggested that NRT should be offered in pregnancy to heavy smokers who cannot stop without it. This is currently not advocated in the UK, but a research evaluation of such a programme should be undertaken.

Combined Pharmacological and Psychological Treatments

5.14   The AHCPR guidelines[84] recommend that both behavioural and pharmacological treatments for smoking cessation are effective components of smoking cessation treatment and should be combined. Buck et al.[95] noted that these treatments provide a high degree of cost effectiveness. When nicotine replacement therapy is offered free or at reduced cost, prescriptions are more likely to be dispensed, use increases and cessation rates improve.

Research - Published Studies and Future Plans

5.15   Computerised expert systems with assessment and individualised feedback have been developed, based on the transtheoretical model of change (Prochaska, Di Clementi 1983;[96] Velicer at al., 1993[97]). This model is so called because elements of several psychological theories on human behaviour are combined. Studies of the way in which individuals had successfully changed undesirable behaviours demonstrated a pattern of progression along a pathway through stages described as pre-contemplation, contemplation, preparation, action and maintenance. Relapse was common and often a number of attempts were needed before lasting behaviour change was achieved. Prochaska and colleagues advocate the tailoring of interventions to the individual's "stage of change" and describe processes necessary to move an individual along the pathway. Preliminary data indicate that such systems, which adjust the intervention to the needs of the individual smoker, can increase long-term abstinence rates over traditional self-help methods. The Committee was informed of four proposed randomised controlled trials (RCTs) in the West Midlands which will be using adaptations of Prochaska's materials and expert computer systems.

5.16   The efficacy of aversion therapy, sensory deprivation and hypnosis are unproven. These methods may warrant further research.

Conclusions

5.17   There is evidence that advice on smoking cessation from health care professionals is effective and worthwhile.

5.18   Nicotine replacement offers a useful and effective adjunct to advice and increases cessation rates.

5.19   Nicotine replacement therapy has not been evaluated in pregnancy.

Recommendations

5.20   Smoking cessation interventions by health care professionals are worthwhile and should be encouraged.

5.21   The timing and nature of advice provided by doctors and midwives to pregnant smokers should be standardised and the effectiveness of such measures should be evaluated.

5.22   Nicotine Replacement Therapy is recommended to reduce withdrawal symptoms and improve cessation rates in smokers who are motivated to give up.

5.23   Consideration should be given to ways of increasing the availability of NRT products including via General Sales List and National Health Service prescriptions.

5.24   A randomised controlled trial is needed on the efficacy and safety of nicotine replacement therapy for pregnant women who smoke heavily and are unable to give up smoking with current advice and support.

5.25   Research is needed on the efficacy and safety of the long term use of NRT as a harm - reduction agent for smokers unable to quit.

PART SIX

MISCELLANEOUS TOPICS _____

Introduction

In addition to considering the major tobacco-associated illnesses such as chronic obstructive pulmonary disease, arterial disease and lung cancer, the Committee has also assessed a number of other tobacco-associated effects and conditions which are brought together in this section.

6.1 The Effect of Smoking on Cognitive Performance and Mood

6.1.1   Many smokers claim that they smoke to alleviate boredom and fatigue, reduce tension, increase concentration and aid relaxation. Furthermore, it has been suggested that smoking confers psychological benefits and that a major motivation for many smokers is the use of smoking as a means of obtaining desired psychological effects, primarily enhancement of cognitive performance or reduction of negative influences such as anxiety, impulsive anger or other adverse situations.[98]

6.1.2   In order to explore some aspects of this widely held belief, the Committee received a presentation on the effect of smoking on cognitive performance and mood.

Cognitive Performance

6.1.3   Data from the Health and Lifestyle Survey[99] were presented. Results of a simple reaction time test showed that cigarette smokers have shorter reaction times than non-smokers or ex-smokers. No dose response effect among smokers was demonstrated. More sophisticated tests assessing choice reaction time, verbal memory and spatial processing showed no difference between smokers, non-smokers and ex-smokers. These results contrast markedly with the results of studies on caffeine intake, where a clear dose response is demonstrated. From these data it can be concluded, therefore, that nicotine has no clear performance enhancing effect.

Mood

6.1.4   Further data from the Health and Lifestyle Survey were considered in which adults completed the General Health Questionnaire, which is a measure of current psychological well being. Results showed that smokers felt worse than never- or ex-smokers and a clear dose response effect was demonstrated, with heavy smokers feeling worst of all.

6.1.5   A malaise questionnaire was completed by subjects in the National Child Development Cohort Study[100] at ages 23 and 33 years. The malaise questionnaire is scored on a continuum from 0-24, with 24 being the most unhappy. Results showed progressive unhappiness with the number of cigarettes smoked and that the risk of current psychiatric disorder increased with increasing cigarette consumption. The results were most striking in women. When confounding factors such as unemployment were eliminated, the relationship between a high malaise score and smoking persisted. Between the two phases of the study malaise scores fell among those who had given up smoking but remained high in those who continued to smoke. Malaise scores were highest of all in those taking up smoking in the period between the two phases of the study.

6.1.6   The conclusion, that smokers do not do better in performance tests nor do they score more favourably on measures of well being, runs counter to commonly held views. Giving up smoking is associated with a reduction in malaise score. It appears that tolerance develops to the mood and performance enhancing effects of cigarettes, with habitual smokers maintaining their habit in order to avert negative mood and performance states. The evidence that smoking relieves stress is weak; rather the reverse is true.[101]

Conclusions

6.1.7   In habitual smokers, nicotine does not appear to enhance performance above non-smoker levels.

6.1.8   In spite of widespread perceptions to the contrary, stress and anxiety are reduced rather than increased after giving up smoking.

6.1.9   The evidence that smoking relieves stress is weak; rather the reverse is true.

Recommendation

6.1.10   The public should be made aware of the association between smoking and negative mood states.

6.2   Smoking and Cancers of the Mouth and Pharynx

6.2.1   Each year in the UK there are more than 2500 new cases of cancers of the mouth and pharynx and, annually, about 1400 people die as a result of developing these tumours.[102] The incidence of oral and pharyngeal cancers was reasonably static in the 1980s but recent reports from several western countries suggest that oral cancers are becoming more common among women and younger patients.[103] The 5- and 10- year survival rates from the time of diagnosis are poor, particularly for large tumours, and early recognition and treatment are critical.

6.2.2   The principal risk factors for this group of tumours in the UK are smoking tobacco and drinking large amounts of alcohol.[9,51,104.105] Chewed tobaccos, which vary widely in form and composition in different parts of the world, are sources of potent carcinogens in the mouth but these and similar materials - notably betel quid - are rarely used in this country except by certain ethnic minority groups. Smoked tobacco and alcohol exert their carcinogenic effects interactively, although it is uncertain whether the interactive effects are additive or multiplicative. It is difficult to evaluate the contribution made by each factor alone as most epidemiological studies are based on patients who both smoke tobacco and drink alcohol, often in large amounts. Relatively few patients with oral and pharyngeal cancers only smoke or only drink alcohol.

6.2.3   For cancers of the mouth and pharynx (and also larynx and oesophagus), alcohol appears to play the dominant role in the alcohol-tobacco synergy. The additional carcinogenic effects of tobacco are, however, consistent and show a dose response effect: the risks of alcohol-related cancers in the head and neck rising in proportion to the amount of tobacco smoked. Cancers of the lip, which are now rare in the UK are something of an anomaly. Traditionally associated with pipe smoking,[106] this tumour develops almost invariably on the lower lip where the hot pipe stem is habitually held between the teeth. Cigarette smoking is also associated with an increased risk of cancers of the lip, and an additional important factor is chronic exposure to UV light. There is no clear association with alcohol consumption.

6.2.4   When deaths from cancers of the oral cavity and cancers of the uterine cervix are compared, the totals for both are similar. In England and Wales in 1996 the figures were 1142 (oral cavity) and 1329 (cervix).[107] There has been intensive screening for cervical cancer for several years but much less attention has been paid to the need to screen for cancers of the oral cavity and pharynx, most of which can be detected by simple inspection.

Conclusions

6.2.5   Many cancers of the mouth and pharynx are caused by smoking tobacco and drinking excessive amounts of alcohol, the effect of the two factors together being greater than the sum of each alone.

6.2.6   Oral cancer, in particular, can be easily detected and early treatment is successful.

Recommendations

6.2.7   The National Screening Committee should consider screening programmes for early detection of cancers in the mouth.

6.2.8   Mandatory training and updating courses, in the detection of oral cancers, should be organised for dental surgeons and dental hygienists.

6.2.9   Consideration should be given to the re-introduction of dental health checks.

6.2.10   Health education should include information about the increased risk in smokers of these cancers

6.3 The Effect of Smoking on Tooth Loss.

6.3.1 The association between smoking and gum disease is an issue of increasing interest and importance, not only to dental practitioners, but to other health professionals and members of the public. In some parts of the world dental practitioners are already very active in raising awareness of the contribution smoking makes to gum disease.[108]

6.3.2 Gum disease starts with gingivitis (inflammation where the gum meets the tooth) which is in turn related to plaque formation. Gingivitis may lead to periodontitis, a condition where the gum comes away from the tooth due to destruction of the underlying bony support. Gum disease is a common cause of tooth loss in later life.

6.3.3 Whilst the development of gingivitis is, to some extent, an inevitable consequence of poor dental hygiene, progression to periodontitis is less predictable. Certain diseases such as diabetes increase the likelihood of serious gum disease, and periodontitis becomes more severe with increasing age. It is now widely accepted that smoking plays a major part in the development of periodontitis and a large study carried out in the United States in 1983[109] showed smoking as an independent risk factor for the development of this disease.

6.3.4 Smoking is important in the evolution of gum disease because it masks the early warning signs of the disease. A comparison of smokers and non-smokers with the same amount of plaque shows smokers to have less inflammation and bleeding than non-smokers. Under normal circumstances bleeding from the gums is an early warning sign that something is wrong, but this is reduced in smokers due to the effect of nicotine, which reduces bleeding. By diminishing this early sign of gingivitis, smoking may delay its recognition to the point where periodontitis sets in and the likelihood of returning to a healthy state is reduced.

Conclusions

6.3.5 Smoking plays a major part in the development of periodontitis, which is the major cause of tooth loss.

6.3.6 Smoking masks the early warning signs of the disease.

6.3.7 Dental surgeons and dental hygienists can play an important role in providing information to the general public on the known health risks of smoking including those associated with dental disease.

Recommendations

6.3.8 The public should be made aware of the role of smoking in the development of gum disease and subsequent tooth loss.

6.3.9   Dentists and dental hygienists should be trained in smoking cessation techniques and encouraged to play an active part in smoking cessation and health education on known health risks of smoking including those associated with dental disease.

6.4   Smoking and Congenital Defects

Orofacial clefts

6.4.1   The role of maternal smoking during pregnancy and a possible association with orofacial clefts has been investigated in studies such as that by Kallen[110] who found a statistically significant association (OR 1.29, 95% CI: 1.08-1.54) with maternal smoking and cleft palate alone and an OR of 1.16 (95% CI: 1.02-1.32) for cleft lip with or without cleft palate. A meta-analysis was carried out by Wyszynski et al[111] which gave a combined OR from 11 studies of 1.29 (95% CI: 1.18-1.42) for cleft lip and palate, and for cleft palate alone gave an OR of 1.32 (95% CI: 1.10-1.62). The authors concluded that their analyses suggest a small but statistically significant association between maternal cigarette smoking in the first trimester of gestation and increased risk of having a child with cleft lip and/or cleft palate.

Congenital Limb Defects

6.4.2   In July 1994 the Committee considered a paper[112] setting out the results of a case control study which examined genetic and environmental factors in the origin of isolated congenital limb deficiencies. The paper concluded that maternal smoking during the first trimester of pregnancy may raise the relative odds for terminal transverse limb deficiencies. (Relative odds 1.48; 95% CI: 0.98-2.23). A recent study from Sweden[113] identified a similar modest increase in the odds ratio for limb-reduction in the babies of women who smoke in pregnancy. (OR 1.26, 95% CI: 1.06-1.50)

6.4.3   Members concluded that there may be an increased risk of congenital limb abnormalities associated with smoking during pregnancy but more research is needed.

Craniosynostosis

6.4.4   Members noted a paper[114] analysing data from a population based case control study to determine whether maternal prenatal smoking or alcohol drinking might increase the risk of craniosynostosis. This paper concluded that maternal prenatal smoking may increase the risk of craniosynostosis in the study population.

Conclusion

6.4.5   Maternal smoking in pregnancy may increase the risk of congenital defects. Prevention may require smoking cessation before conception.

Recommendations

6.4.6   The public should be kept aware of the known hazards of smoking in pregnancy.

6.4.7   Further work on smoking in pregnancy and congenital defects is needed.

6.5   Diseases with a Lower Risk in Smokers

6.5.1   There is evidence that smoking reduces the risk of a few diseases and these findings need to be weighed against the substantial harm.

6.5.2   Members reviewed the current evidence on the effects of smoking in relation to Parkinson's Disease, endometrial cancer, ulcerative colitis and Alzheimer's Disease. A paper was prepared for the Committee by Sir Richard Doll and is attached at **Annex J.**

6.5.3   With respect to Parkinson's disease, endometrial cancer and ulcerative colitis smoking exerts a protective effect which appears to relate to nicotine.

6.5.4   The effect of smoking on Alzheimer's disease is more complicated and studies linking a reduced risk of the disease with smoking habits may demonstrate statistical bias because, for example, younger sufferers may have already been screened out of case control studies by smoking related mortality. Consequently it cannot be concluded that smoking reduces the risk of acquiring Alzheimer's disease.

6.5.5   It is important to recognise that any "beneficial health effects" derived from smoking are far out-weighed by the detrimental effects on health. There are likely to be more than one hundred times as many deaths due to smoking than prevented by smoking. Any beneficial effects are likely to be attributable to nicotine rather than to smoking.

Conclusion

6.5.6   The health benefits of active smoking in a few conditions are far outweighed by the substantial risks.

Recommendation

6.5.7   The apparent beneficial effects of smoking on a few aspects of health offer an opportunity for research on the precise mechanisms involved, and the possibility for developing new pharmaceutical approaches to treatment.

PART SEVEN

TECHNICAL ADVISORY GROUP

Technical Advisory Group – Work Programme

7.1   The Technical Advisory Group (TAG) has conducted a review of emissions from cigarettes (see below), and has played a major role in selecting a programme of research commisssioned by the Department of Health (DH) and carried out by the Laboratory of the Government Chemist (LGC). Members of the TAG have made toxicological assessments of proposed additives in order that they might be used or excluded from use in tobacco products. The TAG has prepared guidelines for a Voluntary Agreement with the tobacco industry on the approval and use of new additives, which are described in **Part Eight**. A full version is to be found at **Annex K**. A review of the procedures used by European and US bodies responsible for food and tobacco regulation was conducted. The group agreed that, although the approval of additives for use in food provided useful toxicological information, data on volatility and the products of pyrolysis were required before permission could be granted for use of an additive in tobacco products.

Laboratory of the Government Chemist

7.2   Yields of various harmful constituents of tobacco smoke have been measured by the LGC on behalf of the DH. Tar, nicotine and carbon monoxide (TNCO) yields are currently measured on a routine basis in accordance with section 9 of the Tobacco Products Labelling (Safety) Regulations, 1991. Yields of some other components of mainstream tobacco smoke which may be hazardous to health have also been determined by the LGC. Assessments of tobacco specific nitrosamines,[115] benzene, nitric oxide (NO) and polycyclic aromatic hydrocarbons (PAHs) have been carried out since 1994. Papers on benzene, NO and PAHs are being be prepared for publication. The LGC have also carried out a study on yields of TNCO and other analytes from cigarettes made from hand-rolling tobacco[116] and are currently determining yields of TNCO, PAHs and benzene from small cigars. Results of the research programme are regularly reported to TAG.

Review of Emissions

7.3   For more than 20 years the Government has taken action to encourage smokers to stop smoking and non-smokers not to start. At the same time a programme of product modification has allowed smokers, unable to give up, to smoke products with lower emissions of noxious substances. At the request of the Scientific Committee on Tobacco and Health, its Technical Advisory Group undertook a review of emissions in cigarette smoke, updating former work. The full text of this review forms **Annex L.**

Tar

7.4   The tar content of cigarette smoke is the single most important factor in terms of health risk. Tar yields of UK manufactured cigarettes have fallen over the past few decades, partly as a result of a programme of cigarette modification and partly in response to legislation. Manufacturers have tended to reduce tar yields in all brands - not just those at the top end of the tar range - and there is growing evidence of increasing consumer acceptance of this trend with more people than ever in 1994 smoking low tar brands.

7.5   Lower tar cigarettes still carry substantial health risks, and there is evidence that smokers largely compensate for lowered yields by increasing inhalation. There is, however, reasonably good evidence to show that lower tar cigarettes are associated with a reduced risk in some smoking related diseases, notably lung cancer. It remains true that tar reduction is no substitute for the avoidance of cigarettes. It is a cause for concern that benefits derived from the increasing popularity of low tar manufactured brands are partly off set by an increase in the smoking of hand-rolled tobaccos in which the tar content is high.

7.6   Yields of nicotine and carbon monoxide in hand rolling tobacco are also higher on average than those from manufactured cigarettes. The TAG recommends that the public should be made aware of the relatively high yields of hand rolling tobacco and of the potential impact of this on health.

7.7   The European Directive to reduce cigarette tar yields to 12 mg should be achieved by January 1998.

Nicotine

7.8   The role of nicotine in the pathogenesis of smoking related diseases is uncertain, although it is clearly implicated in the establishment and maintenance of the smoking habit.[113] Nicotine yields in manufactured cigarettes are not currently controlled, but yields have tended to fall as tar levels have reduced and this trend needs to be maintained.

7.9   The TAG agreed that continuing information is required on the role of nicotine in relation to health and disease. Much work has been done on compensatory smoking.[114]

7.10   The TAG noted the recent settlement negotiated between the US tobacco companies and Attorneys General from forty states[80] and the confirmation of the FDA's authority to regulate tobacco products under the Food, Drug and Cosmetic Act and to regulate the levels of nicotine in these products. The widespread concerns that the settlement undermines the FDA's authority to regulate nicotine were also noted. Nicotine could not be banned from tobacco for 12 years and nicotine levels could not be reduced until the FDA could show substantial evidence of a "substantial reduction on the health risks" and that the nicotine reduction would not create a black market for cigarettes with a high nicotine content.

Carbon Monoxide

7..11   The carbon monoxide (CO) yield from cigarettes has decreased over the past few years, but at a slower rate than tar. As further measures to reduce tar yields are likely to result in similar reductions in CO no specific action is required, although the ratio of yield of CO to tar should be kept under review. The health effects of CO, especially in relation to ischaemic heart disease, are less clear.

Nitrogen and Carbon Derived Noxa

7.12   Yields of nitrogen derived noxa (harmful compounds), such as nitric oxide (NO), relate to the type of tobacco and its nitrate content and are independent of tar yields. Yields of carbon derived noxa, such as polycyclic aromatic hydrocarbons (PAHs), follow those of tar reasonably closely. Tobacco blends containing air-cured tobacco are relatively rich in nitrates and are popular in the United States. Flue-cured tobacco, favoured in the UK, contains higher levels of carbon derived noxa.

7.13   Nitric oxide is produced by the decomposition of nitrates in tobacco and is inhaled by the smoker. Exhaled NO, and NO contained in side stream smoke, gradually oxidise to nitrogen dioxide. Nitrogen dioxide is a respiratory irritant; inhaled NO appears to have no direct toxic effect, although recent research suggests that smoking may adversely affect the physiological function of naturally occurring NO in the lung. Like CO, NO is reduced by increasing cigarette ventilation and paper porosity - measures which also help to reduce tar yield.

7.14   The inverse relationship between the nitrogen and carbon derived noxa from tobacco is well established. Experimental data show that tar from cigarettes made from nitrate rich tobacco, containing reduced yields of PAHs, may be less carcinogenic than tobacco rich in carbon and low in nitrate, suggesting a potential "health benefit" from smoking nitrate rich tobacco. However, the issue is not straightforward, as tobacco rich in nitrate yields higher levels of certain tobacco - specific N-nitroso compounds which are carcinogenic.

7.15   The issue is complex and the TAG concluded that the impact of tobacco type and blend on the genesis of smoking related disease would benefit from further evaluation, together with an examination of the behavioural differences noted in populations smoking cigarettes made from different tobacco blends, to determine what factors, if any, contribute to differences in the incidence and prevalence of smoking related disease.

7.16   Recent studies carried out by the LGC have indicated that yields of NO from cigarettes and hand-rolling tobacco have increased in the last decade. Further work is necessary to establish the reasons for this increase. Total levels of nitrates in tobacco are currently being determined by the LGC in order to assess whether this might be responsible.

Conclusions

7.17   Reduction in tar yields has contributed modestly to reduction in mortality from some diseases caused by smoking, particularly lung cancer.

7.18   Tar reduction is no substitute for not smoking since low tar cigarettes continue to carry important health risks.

7.19   The yields of tar, nicotine, some N-nitroso compounds and carbon monoxide from hand-rolling tobacco are higher on average than those from manufactured cigarettes.

7.20   Nicotine has been shown conclusively to be addictive.

Recommendations

7.21   A policy of further tar reduction in manufactured cigarettes should be pursued without compromising the message of the importance of not smoking.

7.22   As a consequence of potential tar reductions, and thus changes to the manufacturing processes, the monitoring of tar, nicotine and carbon monoxide levels should continue. There should also be investigation into changes in harmful compounds as manufacturing processes change.

7.23   The public should be made aware of the relatively high yields of harmful compounds in hand rolling tobacco and of their potential impact on health.

7.24   There is a continuing need for population studies, such as the Health Survey for England, which relate tobacco type and yield, smoking behaviour and intake and the incidence and prevalence of tobacco related diseases.

7.25   Consideration should be given to smoking status being recorded as part of the death registration process, to aid monitoring of the evolving epidemic of tobacco related diseases.

PART EIGHT

VOLUNTARY AGREEMENT FOR THE APPROVAL OF NEW ADDITIVES TO TOBACCO PRODUCTS

8.1   The inclusion of additives, usually in the form of flavouring compounds to manufactured brands of tobacco products, has played a significant part in the tobacco modification programme over the last few years. One of the effects has been the maintenance of "taste" as tar yields have fallen with an ensuing reduction in natural flavour. The negative side of this has been the maintenance of the appeal of a product, which might otherwise have been rendered unacceptable through the adulteration of intrinsic flavour.

8.2   The scrutiny of additives to tobacco products rests with the Department of Health, which acts on behalf of the UK Health Departments, taking advice from the Scientific Committee on Tobacco and Health and its Technical Advisory Group. This system ensures that smokers are not unwittingly exposed to substances which cause deleterious health effects.

8.3   During 1994 it became clear that the guidelines for the approval of additives to tobacco products, and the arrangements for considering submissions, needed to be revised to take account of scientific and technical advances made since the drawing up of the last agreement, and to ensure the efficient and timely processing of requests for approval.

8.4   Revised guidelines for the approval of new additives to tobacco products and the Voluntary Agreement supporting these guidelines are set out in **Annex K**. These replace guidelines on additive testing set out in Appendix VI of the Second Report of the Independent Scientific Committee on Smoking and Health and the Voluntary Agreement on Tobacco Modification and Research of 22nd March, 1984.

8.5   Following European agreement the document was signed in March 1997 by the representatives of the tobacco manufacturers and importers and the four United Kingdom Health Departments.

Recommendations

8.6   The use of additives in tobacco products should continue to be closely monitored.

8.7   The Technical Advisory Group should regularly review the changing patterns and types of additives.

PART NINE

FUTURE PERSPECTIVES

In this section of the Report the Committee wishes to identify certain topics where recent research is suggesting new health effects of smoking. Mention is made of the putative association between paternal smoking and childhood cancers and also the changes in histological patterns in lung tumours. The introduction of bupropion as a new therapeutic aid to smoking cessation is recorded. New developments relating to the declared content of tobacco, and regulation of its use, are briefly noted and then the section closes with a mention of recent research on nicotine receptors.

Paternal Smoking and Childhood Cancers

9.1   A putative association between cancer in children and paternal smoking at the time of their conception has been proposed in studies based on the Oxford Survey of Childhood Cancers[119,120,121] and a large case-control investigation from Shanghai.[122] The Committee examined the published papers. Certain limitations were noted, but it was agreed that there were plausible hypothetical mechanisms whereby paternal smoking at the time of conception could induce an increase in cancers in the offspring. It is therefore important that future developments in this area are followed.

Changes in Histological Patterns in Lung Tumours of Smokers

9.2   Changes in the incidence of lung cancer in several parts of the world have been accompanied by corresponding changes in their histological type. Squamous and small cell carcinomas, arising from the larger bronchi, are traditionally associated with smoking, but relative and absolute increases in the incidence of adenocarcinomas of the lung have been increasingly recognised. A recent study from Switzerland[123] demonstrates rising incidence rates for adenocarcinomas in both younger men and women in the early 1990s, the rates being more than 3-fold higher than for squamous carcinomas in the same groups. This alteration in histological pattern almost certainly reflects changes in the pattern of exposure of bronchial tissues to tobacco-associated carcinogens. Smokers of modern low-tar filtered cigarettes tend to compensate by increasing the number and depth of puffs, the peripheral parts of the lung are thus more exposed to larger amounts of tobacco-associated carcinogens, and it is in the peripheral parts of the lung that adenocarcinomas develop. The diagnostic and therapeutic implications of an increase in lung adenocarcinomas are likely to be considerable.

New Pharmacological Aid to Smoking Cessation

9.3   A potentially important development in pharmacological aids to smoking cessation has been the recent approval in the USA of the anti-depressant drug bupropion. Preliminary data from clinical trials indicate that bupropion, whose mode of action in not well understood, possesses efficacy as an aid to cessation, and that its combination with nicotine patches works better than either drug alone. This opens up intriguing possibilities for research into brain mechanisms underlying nicotine addiction and for further work to test effects on ongoing smoking and withdrawal.

Tobacco Product Information and Regulation

9.4   The Committee had often expressed concern that smokers were not given detailed information about the constituents of tobacco smoke. They were therefore pleased to note the undertaking, given by the European Commission at the Health Council meeting in December 1997, that the Labelling Directive and the Tar and Nicotine Content Directive would be reviewed.

9.5   In the United States the Food and Drug Administration has recently been given authority to regulate tobacco as a drug. This raises important questions about possible action to regulate tar (or specific tar components), nicotine and gas phase emissions from cigarettes, as well as allowing competition on a more rational basis between the pharmaceutical industry and the tobacco manufacturers. Currently the pharmaceutical industry is strictly regulated in respect of preparations of nicotine and other novel nicotine delivery devices whereas the tobacco industry can launch a new cigarette with the minimum of controls. These issues need consideration in the UK, including the possible establishment of a regulatory authority to control nicotine and tobacco products.

Nicotine receptor research

9.6   Research reported recently in Nature,[124] has provided strong evidence that a particular subtype of the high-affinity neuronal nicotinic acetylcholine receptor is critical to the reinforcing properties of nicotine. Genetically altered mice lacking the beta 2 subunit of this receptor showed little desire to self-administer nicotine. This discovery might in future lead to the possibility of new pharmacological approaches to the treatment of nicotine addiction.

REFERENCES

1.   Office for National Statistics.   *Living in Britain: Preliminary results from the 1996 General Household Survey.* ONS, 1997. London: The Stationery Office.

2.   Health Education Authority. London, December 1996. Unpublished.

3.   Peto R, Lopez A D, Boreham J et al. *Mortality from Smoking in Developed Countries 1950-2000.* Oxford: ICRF and WHO. Oxford University Press, 1994.

4.   World Health Organisation. *Investing in Health Research and Development. Report of the ad-hoc committee on health research relating to future intervention options.* Geneva: WHO, 1996.

5.   Phillips A N, Wannamethee S G, Walker M et al. Life Expectancy in men who have never smoked and those who have smoked continuously: 15 year follow up of large cohort of middle aged British men. *BMJ* 1996; **313:** 907-8

6.   Doll R, Peto R, Wheatley K et al. Mortality in relation to smoking: 40 years' observation on male British doctors. *BMJ* 1994; **309:** 901-11.

7.   Parish S, Collins R, Peto R et al. Cigarette smoking, tar yields, and non-fatal myocardial infarction: 14,000 cases and 32,000 controls in the United Kingdom. The International Studies of Infarct Survival (ISIS) Collaborators. *BMJ* 1995; **311:** 471-7.

8.   Lynch B and Bonnie R, eds. *Growing Up Tobacco Free: Preventing Nicotine Addiction in Children and Youths.*   Institute of Medicine, National Academy Press, Washington, DC: 1994; 3.

9.   Sir Richard Doll and Sir John Crofton, eds. *British Medical Bulletin: Tobacco and Health.* London: The Royal Society of Medicine Press, 1996; (vol 52).

10.   Department of Health. *The Health of the Nation: A strategy for Health in England.* London: HMSO 1992.

11.   Social Services Division of the Office for National Statistics. *Infant Feeding 1995.* London: The Stationery Office, 1997.

12.   Health Education Authority. *Trends in smoking and pregnancy 1992-1997.* London: HEA, 1997.

13.   Office for National Statistics. *Smoking among secondary school children.* London: ONS, 1997. (First Release; ONS (97) 183).

14.   Welsh Office NHS Directorate. *Stategic intent and direction for the NHS in Wales.* Cardiff, 1989. (Copies available from the Welsh Office).

15.   Health Promotion Authority for Wales. *Health for all in Wales: health promotion challenge for the 1990s.* Cardiff: Health Promotion Authority for Wales, 1990.

16.   Health Promotion Authority for Wales. *Technical Report no.27.* Cardiff: Health Promotion Authority for Wales,1998.

17.   Welsh Office Health Department. *New Strategic Plans.* DGM(97) 50. Cardiff: Welsh Office, 1997.

18.   Scottish Office. *Scotland's health: a challenge to us all: a policy statement.* Edinburgh: Scottish Office, 1992.

19.   Scottish Office Home & Health Department. *Health education in Scotland: a national policy statement.* Edinburgh: Scottish Office, 1991.

20.   Scottish Office Home & Health Department, University College London Department of Epidemiology. *Scottish health survey 1995.* Edinburgh: The Stationery Office, 1997.

21.   Office for National Statistics. *Smoking among secondary school children in 1994: Scotland.* London: The Stationery Office, 1995.

22.   Department of Health and Social Services, Northern Ireland. *A Regional Strategy for the Northern Ireland Health and Personal Social Services 1992-1997. Belfast:* DHSS Northern Ireland, 1991.

23.   Northern Ireland Statistics and Research Agency. *Continuous Household Survey 1994/95.* Belfast: Northern Ireland Statistics and Research Agency, 1996.

24.   The Health Promotion Agency for Northern Ireland. *The Health Behaviour of School Children in Northern Ireland: Report of the 1994 Survey.* Belfast: The Health Promotion Agency for Northern Ireland, 1995.

25.   Department of Health and Social Services, Northern Ireland. *Regional Strategy for Health and Social Wellbeing 1997-2002.* Belfast: Department of Health and Social Services Northern Ireland, 1996.

26.   US Department of Health and Human Services. *The health consequences of smoking: nicotine addiction: a report of the Surgeon General.* Washington DC: US Government Printing Office, 1988. (DHSS Publication No (CDC) 88-8406).

27.   Stolerman I P, Jarvis M J. The scientific case that nicotine is addictive. *Psychopharmacology* 1995; **117:** 2-10.

28.   Pich E M, Pagliusi S R, Tessari M et al. Common neural substrates for the addictive properties of nicotine and cocaine. *Science* 1997; **275:** 83-6.

29.   Corrigal W A, Coen K M. Nicotine maintains robust self-administration in rats on a limited-access schedule. *Psychopharmacology* 1989; **99:** 473-8.

30.   McNeill A D. The development of dependence on smoking in children. *Br. J Addiction* 1991; **86:** 589-92

31.   Russell M A H. Nicotine intake and its control over smoking. In: Wonnacott S, Russell M A H, Stolerman I P (Eds). *Nicotine Psychopharmacology: molecular, cellular and behavioural aspects*. Oxford: Oxford University Press, 1990; 374-418.

32.   Kozlowski L T, Wilkinson A, Skinner W et al. Comparing tobacco cigarette dependence with other drug dependencies. *JAMA* 1989; **261:** 898-901.

33.   US Department of Health & Human Services. *Reducing the health consequences of smoking: 25 years of progress: Surgeon General Report*. Washington DC: US Government Printing Office, 1989. (DHSS publication no (CDC) 89-8411).

34.   Strachan D P. Predictors of death from aortic aneurysm among middle-aged men: the Whitehall Study. *B J Surg*. 1991; **78:** 401-4

35.   Wolf P A, D'Agostino R B, Kannel W B et al. Cigarette smoking as a risk factor for stroke: the Framingham study. *JAMA* 1988; **259:** 1025-9

36.   Kannel W B, Shurtleff D. Cigarettes and the development of intermittent claudication. *Geriatrics*. 1973; **28:** 61-8

37.   MacSweeney S T, Ellis M, Worrell P C et al. Smoking and growth rate of small abdominal aortic aneurysms. *Lancet*. 1994; **344:** 651-2

38.   *Independent Scientific Committee on Smoking and Health: third report*. London: HMSO, 1983.

39.   *Independent Scientific Committee on Smoking and Health: fourth report*. London: HMSO, 1988.

40.   EPA. *Respiratory health effects of passive smoking: lung cancers and other disorders: US Environmental Protection Agency*. Washington: Office of Air and Radiation, 1992. (EPA/600/6-90/006F).

41.   National Research Council. *Environmental tobacco smoke: measuring exposures and assessing health effects*. Washington DC, National Academy Press, 1986.

42.   US Department of Health and Human Services. *The health consequences of involuntary smoking:* a report of the Surgeon General. Washington DC: US Government Printing Office, 1986. (DHSS Pub No. (PHS) 87-8398).

43.   *Effects of passive smoking on health*. Report of the NHMRC Working Party on the effects of passive smoking on health. Canberra: Australia Government Publishing Service, 1987.

44.   Hackshaw A K, Law M and Wald N J. The accumulated evidence on lung cancer and environmental tobacco smoke. *BMJ* 1997; **315:** 980-8.

45.   *Report of the California Environmental Protection Agency*. Sacremento: California Environmental Protection Agency, 1997.

46.   *The health effects of passive smoking: a scientific information paper*. Australia: National Health and Medical Research Council, 1997.

47.   *Environmental tobacco smoke and lung cancer: an evaluation of the risk: report of a European working group.* Trondheim: Trondheim European Working Party, 1996. Chairman: J R Idle.

48.   Redhead C S, Rowberg R E. *Environmental tobacco smoke and lung cancer risk: CRS report to Congress.* Washington DC: Congressional Research Service, Library of Congress, 1995. (report 95-1115).

49.   Armitage A K, Ashford J R, Gorrod J W et al. Forum. Environmental Tobacco Smoke - Is it really a carcinogen? *Med Sci Res* 1997; **25:** 3-7.

50.   Davey Smith G and Phillips A. Passive smoking and health: should we believe Philip Morris's "experts"? *BMJ* 1996; **313:** 929-33.

51.   World Health Organisation. International agency for research on cancer: IARC monographs on the evaluation of the carcinogenic risk of chemicals to humans: Tobacco smoking. IARC, Lyon 1986: 421 (vol 38).

52.   Cook D G, Strachan D P and Ross Anderson H. Systematic quantitative review of the effect of ETS exposure on respiratory health in children. Report to the Department of Health. 1997. [Unpublished]. Also in *Thorax,* 1997-1998. Series of papers: "Health Effects of Passive Smoking". Eds. Britton J R and Weiss S T.

53.   Law M R, Morris J K, Wald N J. Environmental tobacco smoke exposure and ischaemic heart disease: an evaluation of the evidence. *BMJ* 1997; **315:** 973-80.

54.   Kawachi I, Colditz G A, Speizer F E et al. A Prospective Study of Passive Smoking and Coronary Heart Disease. *Circulation* 1997; **95:** 2374-9.

55.   *Passive smoking and outcome of pregnancy.* A Report to the Department of Health from the ALSPAC Study, 1994. [Unpublished].

56.   *The Confidential Enquiry into Stillbirths and Deaths in Infancy. Third Annual Report for 1st January to 31st December 1994.* London: Department of Health, 1996.

57.   Blair P S, Fleming P J, Bensley D et al. Smoking and Sudden Infant Death Syndrome: results from 1993 - 5 case-control study for confidential inquiry into stillbirths and deaths in infancy. *BMJ* 1996; **313:** 195-8.

58.   Godfrey C and Maynard A. Economic aspects of tobacco use and taxation policy. *BMJ* 1988; **297:** 339-43.

59.   Marsh A, McKay S. *Poor smokers.* London: Policy Studies Institute, 1994. (PSI research report; no 771).

60.   Mullins R, ed. *Centre for Behavioural Research in Cancer 1994-1995,* 1996. (Quit evaluation studies; no 8).

61.   Balding J. *Young people in 1996: health related behaviour questionnaire results for 22,067 pupils between the ages of 12 and 15.* Exeter: University of Exeter, Schools Health Education Unit, 1997.

62.   Diamond A and Goddard E. *Smoking among secondary schoolchildren in 1994.* OPCS Social Survey Division. London: HMSO, 1995.

63.   Home Office. *Criminal Statistics England and Wales 1996.* London: TSO, 1997. (Cm 3764).

64.   *Why children start smoking. An enquiry carried out by Social Survey Division of OPCS on behalf of the Department of Health.* HMSO. London. 1990.

65.   *Smoking and the Young. A Report of a working party of the Royal College of Physicians.* London: Royal College of Physicians, 1992.

66.   Roderick P and Townsend J. *The effect of cigarette price on teenage smoking.* Briefing paper for the SCOTH, 1994. [Unpublished].

67.   McNeill A D, Jarvis M J, Stapleton J A et al. Nicotine intake in young smokers: longitudinal study of saliva cotinine concentrations. *Am J Public Health.* 1989; **79:** 172-5.

68.   McNeill A D. The development of dependence on smoking in children. *Br J Addiction.* 1991; **86:** 589-92.

69.   Kersler D A, Barnett P S, Witt A et al. The legal and scientific basis for the FDA's assertion of jurisdiction over cigarette and smokeless tobacco. *JAMA.* 1997; **277:** 405 - 9.

70.   Foulds J and Godfrey C. Counting the cost of children's smoking.   *BMJ* 1995; **311:** 1152-4.

71.   *Tobacco Reporter. Serving the Tobacco Industry Since 1873.* United States. March 1994.

72.   Department of Health. *Effect of Tobacco Advertising on Tobacco Consumption: A Discussion Document Reviewing the Evidence.* Department of Health, 1992.

73.   Durston and Jamrozik, eds. *Tobacco and health 1990: the global war: 7th World Conference on Tobacco and Health.* East Perth: Organising Committee of the Seventh World Conference on Tobacco and Health; 71-80.

74.   Bjartveit K. *Nor J Epidemiol* 1995; **5:** 93-106.

75.   Pierce J P, Lee L and Gilpin E A. Smoking initiation by adolescent girls, 1944 through 1988: an association with targeted advertising. *JAMA* 1994; **271:** 608-11

76.   New Zealand Ministry of Health. *Tobacco Statistics 1996.* Pub. Cancer Society of New Zealand.

77.   Pierce J P and Gilpin E A. A historical analysis of tobacco marketing and the uptake of smoking by youth in the United States: 1890-1977. *Health Psychol* 1995; **14:** 500-8.

78.   Pierce J P, Choi W S, Gilpin E A et al. 1996. Validation of susceptibility as a predictor of which adolescents take up smoking in the United States. *Health Psychol* 1996; **15:** 355-61.

79.   U.S. Department of Health and Human Services. *Preventing Tobacco Use Among Young People: A Report of the Surgeon General.* Centers for Disease Control and Prevention. National Center for Chronic Disease Prevention and Health Promotion, Office on Smoking and Health, 1994.

80.   Internet address: http://www.gate.net/~jcannon/documents/settle.txt

81.   Holland J, McGellis S, Arnold S. *Protective factors in adolescent smoking.* A Report for the Department of Health, 1996. [Unpublished]. Also in Coleman J, ed. Adolescence and Society. *Smoking in Adolescence: images and identities.* London and New York: Routledge, 1998.

82.   Lloyd B, Lucas K. *Why do young girls smoke? A quantative/behavioural study.* A Report for the Department of Health, 1996. [Unpublished]. Also in Coleman J, ed. Adolescence and Society. *Smoking in Adolescence: images and identities.* London and New York: Routledge, 1998.

83.   Law M, Tang J L. An analysis of the effectiveness of interventions intended to help people stop smoking. *Arch Intern Med* 1995; **155:** 1933-41.

84.   US Department of Health & Human Services. *Clinical practice guideline 18: Smoking cessation.* Washington DC: US Government Printing Office, 1996. (Agency for health care policy and reseach; publication no 96-0692).

85.   Silagy C, Ketteridge S. *The effectiveness of physician advice to aid smoking cessation.* (3ed.) Oxford: Update Software, 1997. Lancaster T, Silagy C, eds. Tobacco Addiction Module of the Cochrane Database of Systematic Reviews. The Cochrane Collaboration.

86.   Silagy C, Mant D, Fowler G, Lancaster T. *The effect of nicotine replacement therapy on smoking cessation.* (1 ed). Oxford: Update Software, 1997. Lancaster T, Silagy C, eds. Tobacco Addiction Module of the Cochrane Database of Systematic Reviews. The Cochrane Collaboration.

87.   Russell M A H (1991). The future of nicotine replacement. *British Journal of Addiction* **86:** 653-8.

88   Warner K E, Slade J, Sweanor D T. (1997). The emerging market for long-term nicotine maintenance. *JAMA* **278:** 1087-92.

89.   Russell M A H. Realistic goals for smoking and health: A case for safer smoking. *Lancet* 1974; **1:** 254-8.

90.   Benowitz N.L, Gourlay S.G. Cardiovascular toxicity of nicotine: implications for nicotine replacement therapy. *J Am Coll Cardiol* 1997; **29:** 1422-31.

91.   Hughes J R, Wadland W C, Fenwick J W et al. (1991) Effect of cost on the self-administration and efficacy of nicotine gum: a preliminary study. *Prev Med* 1991; **20:** 486-96.

92   Shiffman S, Gitchell J, Pinney J M et al. "Public health benefit of over-the-counter nicotine medications". *Tobacco Control.* [In press].

93.   Olsen J. Cigarette Smoking in Pregnancy and Fetal Growth. Does the type of tobacco

play a role? *Int J Epidemiol* 1992; **21:** 279-84.

94.   Benowitz N L.   Nicotine Replacement Therapy during Pregnancy. *JAMA*. 1991. **266:** 3174-7.

95.   Buck D, Godfrey C and Raw M.   1997. *Cost Effectiveness of Smoking Cessation Interventions*. Centre for Health Economics, University of York and Health Education Authority.

96.   Prochaska J O and DiClemente C C. Stages and processes of self-change of smoking: Toward an integrated model of change. *J. Cons Clin. Psychol 1983*. **51:** 390-5.

97.   Velicer W F, Prochaska J O, Bellis J M et al. An expert system intervention for smoking cessation. *Addict Behav*. 1993. **18:** 269-90.

98.   Jarvis M. ICRF Health Behaviour Unit, University College London. *The Effects of Tobacco Smoking on Concentration and Performance:* an internal review for the Department of Health. 1994. [Unpublished].

99.   Cox B D, Huppert F A, Whichelow M J, eds. *The health and lifestyle survey: seven years on*. Aldershot: Dartmouth Pub Co, 1993.

100.   Ferri E, ed. *National Child Development Cohort Study: life at thirty three: 5th f o l - low up of national child development cohort*. London: National Children's Bureau, 1993.

101.   Parrott A C. Stress modulation over the day in cigarette smokers. *Addiction* 1995; **90:** 233-44.

102.   Office for National Statistics. Registrars General for Scotland and Northern Ireland.

103.   BDA, HEA 1996. (Oral Cancer Factsheets 1 - 5). Supplement to *Br Dent J*, 1996; **180.**

104.   Brugere J, Guenel P, Lelerc A et al.   Differential effect of tobacco and alcohol in cancer of the larynx, pharynx and mouth. *Cancer 1996;* **57:** 391-5.

105.   World Health Organisation. International agency for research on cancer. IARC monographs on the evaluation of the carcingenic risk of chemicals to humans: Alcohol drinking. IARC, Lyon 1988: (vol 44).

106.   Clemmesen J.   *Statistical studies in malignant neoplasms. 1: review and results*. Copenhagen: Munksgaard, 1995.

107.   Information from Office for National Statistics. Mortality statistics 1996: cause. [Unpublished].

108.   Newton J T and Palmer R M. The role of the dental team in the promotion of smoking cessation. *Br Dent J* 1997; **182:** 353-5.

109.   Ismail I I, Burt B A, Eklund S A. Epidemiological patterns of Smoking and Periodontal Disease in the United States. *J Am Dent Assoc* 1983; **106:** 617-23.

110.   Kallen K. Maternal smoking and orofacial clefts. *Cleft Palate-Craniofacial J* 1997; **34:**

11-14.

111.   Wyszynski D F, Duffy D L and Beaty T H.   Maternal cigarette smoking and oral clefts: a meta-analysis. *Cleft Palate-Craniofacial J* 1997; **34:** 206-10.

112.   Czeizel A E, Kodaj I, Lenz W. Smoking during pregnancy and congenital limb deficiency. *BMJ* 1994; **308:** 1473-6.

113.   Kallen K. Maternal smoking during pregnancy and limb reduction malformations in Sweden. *Am J of Pub Health* 1997; **87:** 29-32.

114.   Alderman B E, Bradley C M, Greene C et al. Increased risk of craniosynostosis with maternal cigarette smoking during pregnancy. *Teratology* 1994; **50:** 13-18.

115.   Boardman M C and Darrall K G. 1994. *Survey of Tobacco Specific Nitrosamines in Mainstream and Sidestream Cigarette Smoke.* London: Department of Health, 1994. [Unpublished].

116.   Darrall K G, Figgins J A. Roll - your - own smoke yields: theoretical and practical aspects. *Tobacco Control.* [In press].

117.   *Wald N and Frogatt P, eds. Nicotine, smoking and the low tar programme.* Oxford: Oxford University Press. 1989

118.   *The Biology of Nicotine Dependence.* Chichester: Wiley, 1990. (CIBA Foundation Symposium 152).

119.   Ji B T, Shu X-O, Linet M S et al. Paternal cigarette smoking and the risk of childhood cancer among offspring of non-smoking mothers. *J Nat Can Inst* 1997; **89**: 238-44.

120.   Sorahan T, Lancashire R J, Prior P et al. Childhood cancer and parental use of alcohol and tobacco. *Ann Epidemiol* 1995; **5:** 354-9.

121.   Sorahan T, Lancashire R J, Hulten M A et al.   Childhood cancer and parental use of tobacco: deaths from 1953 to 1955. *Br. J Cancer* 1997; **75:** 134-8.

122.   Sorahan T, Prior P, Lancashire R J et al. Childhood cancer and parental use of tobacco: deaths from 1971 to 1976. *Br J Cancer* 1997; **76:** 1525-31.

123.   Levi F, Franceschi S, La Vecchia C et al. Lung carcinoma trends by histological type in Vaud and Neuchatel, Switzerland, 1974-1994. *Cancer* 1997; **79:** 906-14.

124.   Picciotto M R, Zoli M, Rimondini R et al. Acetylcholine receptors containing the $\beta2$ subunit are involved in the reinforcing properties of nicotine. *Nature* 1998; **391:** 173-7.

ANNEX A

BACKGROUND TO THE SETTING UP OF THE SCIENTIFIC COMMITTEE ON TOBACCO AND HEALTH

The Independent Scientific Committee on Smoking and Health

The previous Government advisory group on tobacco issues was the Independent Scientific Committee on Smoking and Health (ISCSH), initially formed to examine modifications to the smoking process and tobacco products. It met first in 1973 under the chairmanship of Dr Robert Hunter (the late Lord Hunter of Newington) and in 1975 produced its first report[1] which set out guidelines for the testing of tobacco substitutes and for the testing and use of additives in tobacco products. The Product Modification Programme subsequently failed because the product was unacceptable to smokers.

The second phase of the ISCSH work involved the assessment of "lower risk" cigarettes which manufacturers were developing through product modification, primarily tar reduction. A second report[2] was published in 1979, including a first list of permitted tobacco additives. In 1980 Dr Peter Froggatt (later Sir Peter Froggatt) became the new chairman of the committee and the terms of reference were widened to advise industry as well as Government on the development of lower risk tobacco products. (Terms of reference are attached at **Annex B**). The ISCSH continued until 1991 during which time the third[3] and fourth[4] reports were published. These reports included further evaluation of the Product Modification Programme, assessments of the risks from environmental tobacco smoke and from active and passive smoking during pregnancy. The Fourth Report also included an updated list of permitted additives. The Summary of Recommendations of the fourth report is attached at **Annex C**.

When the terms of appointment of the ISCSH members expired at the end of 1991, the opportunity was taken to restructure the membership and range of activities. Most of the recommendations set out in the Fourth Report had been followed up; in particular new regulations had been introduced under EC Directives to limit the tar yields of cigarettes, and much attention had been given to publicising risks of exposure to environmental tobacco smoke and promoting smoke–free policies in public and work places.

In addition to the ISCSH there had been for some years a Department of Health Committee for Research in Behavioural Aspects of Smoking and Health (CRIBASH). Its terms of reference were set out so as to complement and not overlap those of the ISCSH and a major part of its remit was to promote and assess major surveys of the prevalence, distribution and attitudes to smoking carried out by the Office for Population Censuses and Surveys (OPCS) and other organisations. There were also links with the education and smoking cessation work carried out by the Health Education Authority (HEA). It was considered that there would be advantages in subsuming these behavioural aspects of tobacco use into a restructured committee.

REPORT OF THE SCIENTIFIC COMMITTEE ON TOBACCO AND HEALTH

The Scientific Committee on Tobacco and Health

It is important that the development of policy continues to be based on a comprehensive and authoritative assessment of the scientific evidence. In order to ensure that this takes place it was agreed to set up a new committee under the chairmanship of Professor David Poswillo, comprising experts from a range of medical, scientific and behavioural disciplines concerned with the health effects of smoking, to be known as the Scientific Committee on Tobacco and Health (SCOTH). It was anticipated also that SCOTH would provide advice on carrying through objectives on tobacco use as set out in the Health of the Nation White Paper[5] and followed up in the Department of Health's publication Smoke Free for Health[6].

It was agreed that the new committee should be set up in line with other Expert Advisory Committees providing advice to Ministers through the Chief Medical Officer. The terms of reference of the Committee are set out in **Annex D**. A list of Committee members is set out in **Annex E**.

The Technical Advisory Group

One of the commitments in the Health of the Nation White Paper[5] and taken up in SCOTH's terms of reference, is "to review existing controls on additives and the emission of toxic substances from cigarettes and to provide advice on controls". It was considered that additional technical expertise would be needed to carry out this work and a technical advisory group was therefore established. The Terms of Reference of the Technical Advisory Group (TAG) are set out in **Annex F**. A list of TAG members is set out in **Annex G**.

References

1.   *Independent Scientific Committee on Smoking and Health: first report.* London: HMSO, 1975.

2.   *Independent Scientific Committee on Smoking and Health: second report.* London: HMSO, 1979.

3.   *Independent Scientific Committee on Smoking and Health: third report.* London: HMSO, 1983.

4.   *Independent Scientific Committee on Smoking and Health: fourth report.* London: HMSO, 1988.

5.   *The Health of the Nation: A strategy for Health in England.* Department of Health. London: HMSO, 1992.

6.   Department of Health. *The health of the nation: smoke–free for health: an action plan to achieve the health of the nation targets.* London: Department of Health, 1994.

ANNEX B

TERMS OF REFERENCE OF INDEPENDENT SCIENTIFIC COMMITTEE ON SMOKING AND HEALTH (ISCSH)

The committee is appointed by the Health Ministers to advise them and, where appropriate, the tobacco companies on the scientific aspects of matters concerning smoking and health, in particular:

(a)   **i.**   To receive in confidence full data about the constituents of cigarettes and other smoking materials and their smoke and changes in these.

   ii.   To release to *bona fide* research workers for approved subjects such of the above as is agreed by the suppliers of it.

(b)   To review the research into less dangerous smoking and to consider whether further such research, including clinical trials and epidemiological studies, needs to be carried out;

   and

(c)   to advise the validity of research results and of systems of testing the health effects of tobacco and tobacco substitutes and on their predictive value to human health.

ANNEX C

RECOMMENDATIONS OF FOURTH REPORT OF ISCSH

General Policy

1. It is essential that more smokers are encouraged to stop smoking and that non-smokers are strongly discouraged from starting: Government should consider all options available to them. (para 30)

2. The role of the tar/carbon monoxide/nicotine tables within the framework of anti-smoking policies as a whole, the extent of publicity accorded to them and the layout of information and advice within them should be re-examined in order to achieve the maximum impact. (para 45)

Product Modification

3. The sales weighted average tar yield should be not more than 13 mg/cigarette by the end of 1988 and should continue to decline with a target of 12 mg/cigarette by the end of 1991. (para 12)

4. The tar yields of new brands should continue to be subject to a ceiling defined as the sales weighted average tar yield of the middle and low-to-middle tar brands during the preceding six-month survey period. (para 13)

5. As soon as possible there should be an upper limit of 16 mg tar per cigarette placed on existing brands on sale, reducing to 15 mg after two years and becoming 14 mg for ALL brands after four years. (para 31)

6. While the overall aim should be towards reductions in the tar: nicotine ratio this should not be through the enhancement nor solely through the maintenance of present-day middle range nicotine levels (around 1.3 mg/cigarette). In general the sales weighted average nicotine yields should fall, and on the lines of the suggestion made in our Third Report (para 20) there should continue to be some brands available to the public with nicotine yields below 1 mg and with tar yields reduced to a proportionately greater extent (below 8 mg). (para 34)

7. Manufacturers should take steps to reduce carbon monoxide yields of all brands of cigarettes and the yields of new brands should be subject to a ceiling defined as the sales weighted average carbon monoxide yield of brands in the middle and low-to-middle tar bands during the preceding six-month survey period. (para 20)

8. Government and the tobacco industry should consider what further action could be taken to persuade more smokers to favour low tar brands. (para 33)

Composition and properties of tobacco smoke

9. There should be further investigation of the possibility of short-term tests to predict the carcinogenic activity of smoke from modified products. (para 40)

10. The investigation of yields of other smoke components as identified in the Third report (para 27) in representative cigarette types should continue. (para 43)

11. The Committee should continue to scrutinize all new developments: and in addition to the regular determinations of tar/CO/nicotine carried out by the Laboratory of the Government Chemist, there should be studies in newly emerging products of the composition of particulate and gaseous phases of the smoke and of the effect of different smoking patterns on yields and human uptake. (para 44)

Research Activities

12. Provision should still be made for supporting the epidemiological and other research work needed to examine effects on health of modified products. (para 47)

13. The Commitee should have access to funds enabling it to promote and support investigations into biological effects of smoking in general. (para 49)

Environmental Tobacco smoke (ETS, passive smoking)

14. Further publicity should be given to the risk of lung cancer arising from exposure to other people's tobacco smoke. (para 69)

15. Continued attention should be given to the investigation of the role of environmental tobacco smoke in the occurrence of respiratory illness in children, and to the longer-term sequelae. (para 71)

16. The tobacco industry should pursue research into ways of reducing the amount, irritancy and other deleterious properties of sidestream smoke from all tobacco products. (para 73)

17. Consideration should be given to ways of ensuring that in the work and leisure environments, in public transport and other public enclosed spaces smokers can be segregated from non-smokers. (para 74)

Effects of tobacco smoke on the fetus

18. Further publicity needs to be given to the importance of not smoking during pregnancy and to avoid as practicably as possible exposure to other people's smoke. (para 80)

ANNEX D

SCIENTIFIC COMMITTEE ON TOBACCO AND HEALTH

Terms of Reference

The Committee is appointed to provide advice to the Chief Medical Officer on scientific matters concerning tobacco and health, in particular:

- to review scientific and medical evidence on such areas relating to tobacco and health, including behavioural aspects of tobacco use, as may be agreed between the Committee and the UK Health Departments and in the light of these reviews,

- to advise on research priorities on tobacco and health, including behavioural aspects of tobacco use;

- to provide advice to the Department of Health, acting on behalf of the UK Health Departments, about the constituents of tobacco products and their smoke;

- to review existing controls on additives and the emission of toxic substances from cigarettes and to provide advice on controls.

ANNEX E

MEMBERSHIP OF SCOTH

Professor David Poswillo (Chairman)
Professor emeritus, United Medical and Dental Schools, Guy's & St Thomas's Hospital, London.

Dr Marion Hall
Department of Obstetrics and Gynaecology, Aberdeen Royal Hospitals NHS Trust, Aberdeen.

Professor Roger Greenhalgh
Imperial College of Science and Medicine, Department of Surgery, Charing Cross Hospital, London

Professor Nicholas Wald
Wolfson Institute of Preventive Medicine, St Bartholomew's and The Royal London School of Medicine and Dentistry, London

Professor Richard Peto
Clinical Trial Service Unit and Epidemiological Studies Unit, Radcliffe Infirmary, Oxford University

Dr Martin Jarvis
Imperial Cancer Research Fund Health Behaviour Unit, University College London Medical School, London

Professor David Marks
Middlesex University, London

Professor Richard Carter
Royal Marsden Hospital and University of Surrey

Dr Aidan Macfarlane
Department of Public Health and Health Policy, Oxfordshire Health Authority

Professor Godfrey Fowler
Professor emeritus of General Practice, Oxford University

Professor Robert Curnow
Professor emeritus, Reading University

Observers

Dr A C Peatfield
Medical Research Council (until April 1997)

Dr Debbie Colson
Medical Research Council (from July 1997)

Mr John Day
Laboratory of the Government Chemist

Mrs Cheryl Swann
Tobacco Products Research Trust (set up under ISCSH) and former scientific secretary to ISCSH

Other Health Departments

Dr Barbara Davis
Senior Medical Officer, Scottish Office Department of Health

Dr Bill Smith
Head of Health and Social Policy Unit, Department of Health and Social Services, Northern Ireland

Dr Paul Tromans
Senior Medical Officer, Welsh Office

Department of Health

Professor Frank Fairweather
Scientific Consultant, Toxicologist, former ISCSH member

Mr Robert Waller
Scientific Secretary until July 1996. Former scientific secretary to ISCSH from 1984

Dr Susan Shepherd
Medical Secretary until July 1996

Dr Dawn Milner
Medical Secretary from July 1996

Dr Gillian Shine
Scientific Secretary from August 1996

ANNEX F

SCIENTIFIC COMMITTEE ON SMOKING AND HEALTH TECHNICAL ADVISORY GROUP

Terms of reference:

The Technical Advisory Group is appointed to provide advice to CMO, through the Scientific Committee on Tobacco and Health, on technical aspects relating to tobacco products and their effects on health, in particular:

- to review information on the composition of tobacco and tobacco smoke and to consider proposals for further analytical work

- to follow findings from the routine monitoring of smoke components and to advise on any changes in procedure that may be required

- to review existing controls on additives and the emission of toxic substances from cigarettes and provide advice on controls

- to study information on innovative tobacco products and possible impacts on health effects.

ANNEX G

MEMBERSHIP OF TECHNICAL ADVISORY GROUP

Professor Richard Carter
Royal Marsden Hospital and University of Surrey

Professor Frank Fairweather
Scientific Consultant, Toxicologist. Former ISCSH member.

Professor Tim Higenbottam
Sheffield University Medical School

Dr Martin Jarvis
Imperial Cancer Research Fund, Health Behaviour Unit, University College, London

Mr John McAughey
AEA Technology plc, Harwell

Dr Chris Powell
St Bartholomew's and the Royal London School of Medicine & Dentistry, London

Dr David Purser
Fire Research Station, Building Research Establishment, Garston, Watford

Dr Mary Seller
United Medical & Dental Schools, Guy's & St Thomas's Hospital, London

Dr Stan Venitt
Institute of Cancer Research, London

Observer

Mr Keith Darrall
Laboratory of the Government Chemist

Department of Health

Dr Eileen Rubery
Head of Health Promotion (Medical) Division. Chairman until February 1995

Dr Susan Shepherd
Senior Medical Officer. Chairman from February 1995 until July 1996

Dr Dawn Milner
Senior Medical Officer. Chairman from July 1996

Mr Andy Browning
Scientific Secretary until April 1996

Mr Robert Waller
Scientific Secretary until July 1996.

Dr Gillian Shine
Scientific Secretary from August 1996

ANNEX H

STATEMENT BY THE COMMITTEE ON THE CARCINOGENICITY OF CHEMICALS IN FOOD, CONSUMER PRODUCTS AND THE ENVIRONMENT TO SCOTH ON ENVIRONMENTAL TOBACCO SMOKE (ETS) AND LUNG CANCER

Introduction

1. We have been asked by the Scientific Committee on Tobacco and Health (SCOTH) to review a submission from the Tobacco Manufacturers Association (TMA) comprising a meta–analysis of epidemiological data and supporting references, and a separate meta–analysis paper prepared by Dr A Hackshaw and Professor N Wald (a member of SCOTH). The data provided by the TMA comprised three volumes of reviews and references originally received by the SCOTH secretariat in 1994, and updated in February 1995. A key part of the TMA submission was a meta–analysis of epidemiological studies prepared by Mr P N Lee which was updated in December 1996. The TMA recently submitted 3 additional supplements dated January 1997 dealing with; misclassification bias, dose response (with and without exposed groups), and use of cotinine as a biomarker for exposure to ETS[*]. We considered all of the submitted information at two meetings in 1997. A further meta–analysis report prepared by an ad–hoc European Working Group was also considered.[1] We have also considered additional published literature on the formation and composition of ETS, the results obtained in animal experiments involving exposure to surrogates of ETS, and information regarding investigations to evaluate the potential genotoxicity and biological interactions of ETS in humans published up to June 1997.

2. Smoking tobacco is the predominant cause of lung cancer with approximately 90% of lung cancer deaths in Western populations attributable to cigarette usage.[2,3,4] A lower percentage of lung cancer deaths may be attributed to tobacco smoking in developing non–Westernised populations.[4] A number of epidemiological assessments undertaken by national regulatory agencies have reported a small but statistically significantly elevated relative risk for lung cancer in passive smokers of between 1.1 to 1.3 ,[3,5,6] whereas other reviewers[7–11] concluded that the observed association is due to uncontrolled confounding and biases in these analyses. However, since many individuals within the population are exposed to ETS, it is important to resolve the scientific issues particularly as only a small increase in risk would be associated with many hundreds of deaths due to lung cancer per year.

3. Regarding the structure of our review, it was agreed to consider firstly the nature and composition of ETS followed by information on exposure and uptake of genotoxic components (eg adduct studies) with particular reference to the lung as the target organ.

---

[*]Some abbreviations used throughout this statement. ETS = Environmental Tobacco Smoke, MS = mainstream smoke, SS = side stream smoke, TSNA = Tobacco Specific Nitrosamine. NNK = 4–(methylnitrosamino)–1–(3–pyridyl)–1–butanone. NNN= N–nitrosonornicotine. NB: Throughout this statement the terms "exposure to ETS"and "passive smoking" have been used interchangeably.

Finally to critically review the submitted epidemiological meta–analyses. All of the available information has been evaluated in accordance with our guidelines[12] and also with regard to the criteria proposed by Sir Austin Bradford–Hill.[13]

These latter criteria, which are listed below, are generally regarded as being valuable in the consideration as to whether or not an association between an outcome (in this case lung cancer) and a putative risk factor (passive smoking) is causal.[14] A specific reference to each of these criteria in respect of passive smoking and lung cancer has been included in our discussion.

Bradford–Hill criteria

Strength
Consistency
Specificity
Temporality
Biological gradient
Plausibility
Coherence
Experiment
Analogy

Composition of ETS

4.   An essential part of our evaluation concerned the chemical composition of ETS and a comparison of this information with data on the composition of mainstream smoke (MS). There is extensive literature on the presence of chemicals in smoke from cigarettes and other tobacco products and many reviews of this information are available.[3,4,15–19] ETS consists predominantly of aged diluted sidestream smoke (SS) and some exhaled MS with each type of smoke comprising both a particulate and vapour phase. MS is derived from direct inhalation of smoke from the mouth end of a cigarette whilst SS is the material released directly into the air from the burning tip of the cigarette plus that which diffuses through the cigarette paper. The physical and chemical characteristics of ETS are dynamic and differ significantly from MS and fresh SS. The size of ETS particles decreases rapidly with time due to evaporation of volatile constituents and thus ETS particles are usually smaller than MS particles (ETS particles are approximately 0.1–0.25 μm MMAD whereas MS are approximately 0.1–0.9 μm MMAD).[3,5,15,17,20] The chemical composition of ETS also changes rapidly with aging and dilution.[21] Nicotine, which is tobacco specific, is present predominantly in the vapour phase of ETS (ca 95%) with a relatively small amount in the particulate phase (ca 5%).[3] Concentrations of ETS particulate nicotine rapidly reduce due to evaporation from particles whilst the concentration of nicotine in vapour may reduce due to adsorption onto surfaces.[3,15]

5.   MS has been the subject of extensive investigation and approximately 4,000 chemicals have been identified to date comprising about 95% of the MS weight.[3,4,5] About 10% of these chemicals have been quantified in both MS and SS and these include a lengthy list of known human carcinogens such as 2–naphthylamine, 4–aminobiphenyl, arsenic, hexavalent chromium, vinyl chloride, benzene and a number of genotoxic animal carcinogens that are regarded as potential human carcinogens such as certain polycyclic aromatic hydrocarbons (PAHs, eg benzo(a)pyrene) and nitrosamines (including the Tobacco Specific Nitrosamines (TSNAs) NNK and NNN).[3,4,5,15] Yields per cigarette of

some carcinogens have been reported to be greater in SS compared to MS[22-28] as shown in the table below which presents some selected data from the United States National Research Council (NRC) review.[5] Yields of some individual chemicals including a number of carcinogens present in SS have been reported to be relatively constant between different commercial brands including filter and non filter brands of cigarettes. [22,24,27]

Phase	Amount MS	Ratio SS/MS
Vapour		
Benzene	12-4 μg	2.5-4.7
N-nitrosodimethylamine	10-40 ng	20-100
N-nitrosodiethylamine	ND-25 ng	< 40
N-nitrosopyrrolidine	6-30 ng	6-30
Particulate		
2-Naphthylamine	1.7 ng	30
4-aminobiphenyl	4.6 ng	31
Benzo(a)anthracene	20-70 ng	2-4
Benzo(a)pyrene	20-40 ng	2.5-3.5
N-nitrosonornicotine	100-3,000 ng	0.5-3
NNK	100-1,000 ng	1-4

6.   One Research group documented evidence that the use of filters reduced MS emissions from cigarettes but had little effect on SS emission of a number of carcinogens.[22] Thus some reviewers consider that it is misleading to place too much emphasis on MS/SS ratios.[3,15] However we consider it important to note that the data suggest that all three types of smoke MS, SS and ETS contain the same carcinogens and although there will be quantitative differences in composition between different types of smoke, it is likely that the exposure of active and passive smokers to carcinogens will be qualitatively similar.   A critical review of the available exposure data on ETS with particular consideration of derived doses of carcinogens in the lung (the target tissue) is given below.

Exposure to carcinogens present in ETS

7.   We have considered the available exposure data with particular consideration of the potential exposure of the lung to ETS particles and carcinogens adsorbed to these particles.   Several reviews of ETS exposure studies are available.[3,5,15,17]   The majority of these studies have involved either static or personal monitoring of exposure to carbon dioxide, nicotine, total or respirable particles or ETS particles (estimated by UV or florescence light techniques, or as solanesol particulate material; solanesol is a tobacco leaf

constituent).[3,5,15] There are a number of recent examples of both static monitoring studies[29–33] and personal monitoring studies.[34–36] Fewer investigations have reported data on actual exposures to carcinogens present in ETS in field studies (ie under prevailing ambient conditions without manipulating either smoking or environmental conditions).[3,5,37] However, there are data to show increased concentrations of carcinogens in indoor air either during or following smoking in respect of benzene, polycyclic aromatic hydrocarbons and nitrosamines thus providing some data on exposure to carcinogens from ETS in field studies.[37–41] Some reviewers have commented on the poor control for extraneous non tobacco related sources of carcinogens in the available field studies of indoor air.[15,37] Many of the carcinogens which can be found in indoor air such as benzene, polycyclic aromatic hydrocarbons and some volatile nitrosamines can be derived from several sources other than ETS.[15,43,44] Exposure to these chemicals will vary depending on location (ie at home, work, or at public venues, during transportation or resulting from leisure activities), local environmental conditions such as cooking of foods and ventilation, and air pollution. A limited number of exposure studies have reported increased concentrations of TSNAs in ETS,[15] or in SS.[45] One report has documented increased air concentrations of TSNAs (NNK and NNN) derived from ETS in a variety of situations including restaurants, bars and trains.[40]

8. Quantifying exposure to the carcinogens in ETS and in particular dose levels in the lung is complicated particularly as the chemical composition of ETS rapidly changes depending on factors controlling the levels of MS and SS such as the number of smokers present, the building or room occupation density, size of building/room, number of cigarette or other tobacco products smoked over a given period, individual smoking patterns (puff rate, inhalation volume and duration) and factors controlling losses such as degradation/modification of vapour and particulate ETS constituents through chemical reaction or UV light, and the dilution of ETS constituents due to ventilation, mixing of components (ie homogeneity of ETS) and/or absorption and desorption from surfaces in the room.[3,5,15,17,46–48] To illustrate the high potential for variation in air levels of ETS, the United States National Research Council (NRC) modeled air levels of respirable particles (RSPs, <2.5 μm) for a range of conditions expected to be encountered in private residences with one smoker consuming 1–2 cigarettes per hour and found RSP levels varied by two orders of magnitude from approximately 17–5,000 μg/m^3.[5]

9. A large number of the carcinogens associated with ETS are present in the particulate phase. The fraction of ETS particles deposited in the respiratory tract during passive smoking was reported to be 11 ± 4%, ie lower than the fraction of MS particles deposited in the respiratory tract of active smokers (47% ± 13%).[49,50] Data from the ICRP66 Lung model reported in the Department of Health Committee on Medical Effects of Air Pollutants report on non–biological particles and health suggest that approximately 42% of 0.05 μm particles and 29% of 0.2 μm particles are deposited in the respiratory tract with a significant proportion of these particles reaching the alveoli.[51] These data suggest that ETS particles (ca 0.1–0.25 μm) will penetrate to all regions of the respiratory tract. One group of investigators has calculated that a higher deposition of ETS particles compared to MS particles will occur in the terminal bronchioles and alveoli of the lung.[52] The respiratory epithelium of the human lung contains cells with appropriate metabolising capacity to activate carcinogens associated with ETS particles (for example polycyclic aromatic hydrocarbons,[53] and tobacco specific nitrosamines such as NNK[54]).

10.   Overall we consider that there are sufficient data to conclude that passive smoking results in an increased dose of genotoxic carcinogens to the respiratory tract including the alveolar region of the lung. In the following section we review the available studies which have investigated the biological properties of ETS particles.

Biological properties of ETS

11.   ETS particles contain adsorbed genotoxic carcinogens. The following section presents a review of the biological properties of ETS particles and in particular an assessment of the mutagenic potential of urine samples obtained under field conditions and an evaluation of studies in animals and individuals exposed to ETS. In considering the available studies of the biological properties of ETS, we have paid particular attention to information which is important in assessing whether passive smoking results in exposure to and activation of genotoxic carcinogens in the lung. We have compared exposure data reported in these investigations with published information from field studies[15] in order to evaluate degree of exposure to ETS, although we note that only a limited assessment of exposure is possible.

Mutagenic chemicals adsorbed to particles

12.   Several research groups have used air sampling techniques in field studies to collect ETS particles and similar methods to collect SS particles during exposure studies. Solvent extracts made from these particles tested in bacterial mutagenicity tests showed the presence of adsorbed mutagenic chemicals which were active in both the presence and absence of an exogenous metabolising fraction.[39,55–62] It is difficult to compare the results of the field studies in view of differing methods used in these investigations, the results of which depend heavily on the rate of smoking, sampling methods, number of particles collected by filters, solvent extraction methods, the mutagenicity test methods adopted and the possible influence of confounding sources of air particles containing adsorbed mutagenic substances. Although data regarding objective measures of actual exposures to ETS in these studies were incomplete, we conclude that the weight of evidence supports the view that exposure to mutagenic particles present in ETS occurs under a wide range of field conditions and therefore it is likely to occur under all conditions of passive smoking.[39,57,61]

Studies in animals

13.   Exposure of mice to very high levels of fresh SS is clastogenic inducing micronuclei in polychromatic erythrocytes and exposure of rats to very high levels of either aged diluted or fresh SS induces DNA adducts in a variety of tissues such as the heart, lung, larynx and bladder.[63–66] It has been established that MS is carcinogenic in hamsters and rabbits exposed by inhalation or following the application of MS condensates to the skin of mice and rabbits or intrapulmonary injection in rats.[4] MS condensates may also act as tumour initiators and promoters in animals.[4] SS is carcinogenic in rats when implanted into the lung[67] or in mice following skin application.[68,69] The results of the skin painting studies in mice have also suggested that on a gravimetric basis the carcinogenic potential of SS condensate exceeds that of MS condensate.[68,69] These data show that whole MS and its condensate and SS condensates are carcinogenic in animals and hence we consider it is likely that ETS will also be carcinogenic to animals. However, we note that there are no appropriate life–time bioassays using ETS available to confirm this. We consider that the recent inhalation study where a carcinogenic response was documented in strain A mice exposed to extremely high levels of SS reinforced with some

MS was of very limited value and cannot be used to predict hazards to humans.[70,71] Evidence of reversible hyperplasia and squamous metaplasia in the nasoturbinates accompanied by active chronic inflammation have been documented in short term inhalation studies of aged diluted SS,[72,73] but the relevance of these findings to the potential carcinogenicity of ETS is unclear.

Studies in humans

14.   The biological effects of exposure to ETS have been examined in studies involving the measurement of metabolites of carcinogens and the presence of mutagenic substances in urine from exposed individuals. Other relevant studies have investigated chromosomal aberrations and markers of DNA damage (SCEs) in blood lymphocytes and the detection and quantification of carcinogen adducts with DNA and proteins such as haemoglobin or albumin.[33,45,74–85] It was reported in the previous section of this statement (see paragraphs 7–10) that exposure to ETS occurs by inhalation and ETS particles are deposited throughout the respiratory tract which has the necessary metabolic capability to activate carcinogens present in ETS. We therefore consider that the presence of carcinogens and/or their adducts in blood or urine provides clear evidence of exposure of the lung to the ultimate genotoxic carcinogens.

15.   There is evidence of a small increase in the concentration of mutagenic substances in urine samples taken from passive smokers in a number of investigations where small groups of individuals were exposed to high levels of ETS for periods of 5–8 hours.[78,79,83] Only one of these studies included partial control for dietary confounding which has been reported to affect the excretion of mutagens in the urine of active smokers.[86] A further exposure study where a small group of subjects were maintained on controlled diets did not find a significant increase in the excretion of urinary mutagens following exposure to high levels of ETS for 8 hours.[33,82] Limited evidence of increased urinary excretion of mutagenic substances following exposure to ETS has been documented in a small survey of waiters and waitresses[80] and in a small survey of blood donors.[87] No evidence for an increase in chromosome aberrations in peripheral lymphocytes was documented in one study involving waiters exposed to ETS in restaurants[74] or in a number of investigations which considered sister chromatid exchanges in blood lymphocytes[74,79–81,84]

16.   Some more recent studies examined carcinogen DNA or protein adducts in passive smokers.[33,75–77,81,85] No increase in ^{32}P–postlabelling of DNA was noted in blood monocytes taken from volunteers exposed to high levels of ETS for 8 hours.[33] However, we considered that sampling of blood monocytes was not the most appropriate technique for monitoring exposure to tobacco smoke carcinogens, even in heavy smokers.[88–91] Protein adducts can serve as surrogates for DNA adducts, particularly at low exposure doses[92–94] and thus most recent attention has therefore been focused on the measurements of protein adducts. A short resume of the main results from three critical studies is presented below.

17.   Crawford et al found a statistically significant increase in protein adducts of polycyclic aromatic hydrocarbons using albumin as a marker in children whose mothers smoked compared to children whose mothers did not smoke.[75] We note that elevated plasma cotinine was also found in children whose mothers smoked and consider that this study was adequately performed. MaClure et al measured adducts of 4–aminobiphenyl (4–ABP)and 3–aminobiphenyl (3–ABP) with haemoglobin following hydrolysis to release these aromatic amines. For 4–ABP adducts there was substantial variability in

the results limiting the conclusions that could be drawn. Adducts of 3–ABP were more significantly associated with passive smoking.[76] Hammond et al used the same assay as MaClure et al to examine the levels of 4–ABP haemoglobin adducts in pregnant women. Among non–smokers the levels of 4–ABP adducts increased with exposure to ETS. We have considered the results of this study[77] and the subsequent correspondence relating to it[95-96] and consider that the investigation was adequately conducted and results obtained were valid. It has been demonstrated that 4–ABP exposure in individuals with no history of occupational exposure to this chemical is predominantly derived from tobacco smoking[94] and thus the results obtained by Hammond et al provide good evidence that low level exposure to ETS can result in the absorption of genotoxic carcinogens. In a separate study Hecht et al found increased excretion of urinary 4–(methyl-nitrosamino)–1–(3–pyridyl)–1–butanol (NNAL), a specific marker for exposure to the tobacco specific carcinogen 4–(methylnitrosamino)–1–(3–pyridyl)–1–butanone (NNK) in a small group of 5 individuals exposed to a high level of fresh SS smoke for 3 hours.[45] This study provides good evidence to support the view that passive smoking results in exposure of the respiratory tract to tobacco specific carcinogens.

18. Exposure to ETS over a wide range of exposure levels, including those normally encountered in homes, at work and in public places can lead to the inhalation and delivery of genotoxic carcinogens to all parts of the respiratory tract. Furthermore such compounds will be in contact with cells capable of metabolic activation to produce the proximate carcinogens. These data give rise to concern regarding an increased risk of lung cancer in passive smokers. The available information on passive smokers is consistent with that reported for current cigarette smokers where elevated levels of DNA adducts have been documented in samples of lung tissue.[88,97-102] The COC advice on genotoxic carcinogens is to make the prudent assumption that any exposure may be associated with some increased health detriment.[12] This policy is further supported in this specific instance by the approximately linear dose–response relationship between daily consumption of cigarettes by active smokers and lung cancer risk[14] which we consider is consistent with a lack of a threshold. Thus exposure to ETS may be associated with an increased risk of lung cancer, but it is not possible on the basis of these data to make any estimate of the putative increased risk.

Assessment of submitted meta–analysis reports

19. The epidemiological problems regarding passive smoking are common to the evaluation of the potential association between a low level risk factor and disease. These include the requirement for large numbers of individuals in epidemiological investigations in order for the statistical power of these studies to be acceptable with regard to identifying potential associations, the potential for significant confounding by other risk factors for lung cancer, the possibility of publication bias and misclassification bias, and finally the adequacy of exposure estimation. Some research groups have considered it appropriate to evaluate relative risks of lung cancer in passive smokers by undertaking meta–analyses of the available epidemiological data. We note that the two meta–analyses prepared specifically for SCOTH and reviewed in this statement considered essentially the same studies and that the criteria for inclusion and exclusion were clearly stated. We concur with the specific analyses of publication bias which have concluded this is unlikely to be a factor in passive smoking studies,[103,104] but the potential for dietary confounding, misclassification and measurement error need to be considered. We also note from the meta–analysis reports that there were geographical variations in the rate of misclassification that need to be considered.

20. We have previously considered the role of meta–analysis in the evaluation of cancer epidemiology at a COC symposium involving invited epidemiologists in February 1994 where participants agreed that meta–analysis was an improvement on conventional reviews, although the statistical analysis alone was not helpful without an associated qualitative review (unpublished report). The overall conclusion of the meeting was that a report of a meta–analysis must include 3 stages – a full narrative review, the statistical analysis (random effects and mixed models considered most useful) and careful interpretation of the results. These conclusions are in accordance with published reviews on the conduct, reporting and evaluation of meta–analysis of epidemiological studies of carcinogenesis.[105] We have looked at the meta–analysis reports submitted to us in accordance with these criteria.

Meta–analysis prepared for TMA by PN Lee.

21. The authors considered 44 studies, (39 case–control, 5 prospective). Three case–control studies were of a nested design. Data on smoking were available for 6 categories; husband (n=42), wife (n=13), workplace (n=16), childhood (n= 18), social (n=6), and total ETS exposure (n=15). There was a total of 5220 female non–smoking lung cancer patients and 388 male non–smoking patients considered. The authors noted that almost 80% of studies had not found a statistically significant effect. Meta–analysis was performed using a fixed effects model and the published RR estimates. A significant association was found in the 42 studies which evaluated lung cancer in non–smoking women living with husbands who smoked RR = 1.19 (95% CI 1.10–1.27) unadjusted and 1.16 (95% CI 1.08–1.24) based on published adjusted results. Additional calculations were performed using a random effects model which gave essentially the same estimates RR = 1.22 (95% CI 1.11–1.36) unadjusted and 1.24 (95% CI 1.11–1.39) for adjusted data. The analyses were not adjusted for misclassification bias because the authors noted that this varied considerably between investigations according to culture and situation in which questions were asked. A follow–up analysis which adjusted for misclassification of ever smokers as non–smokers (2.5% for US, Western or European and 10% for Asian studies) was conducted with data from 39 studies and reported that the overall risk estimate was not significant when a concordance ratio of 3 was assumed (RR = 1.06, 95% CI 0.98–1.14). Evidence for a dose response was reported for 10/39 case–control studies. The authors found significant heterogeneity between studies (including geographical, time of study, size of study, and quality of study). Although no heterogeneity by type of study (prospective versus case–control) was reported, the authors did report heterogeneity by type of control group in the case control studies: investigations with hospital or decedent controls had an RR of 1.33 (95% CI 1.16–1.52) compared to an RR of 1.06 (95% CI 0.96–1.16) for studies with general population controls. The authors proposed that misclassification, uncontrolled confounding, publication bias, recall bias, and inconsistencies between cases and controls could explain the weak association and dose response for lung cancer found in non–smoking women living with men who smoked. The authors also noted that there was no statistically significant association between lung cancer and any other exposure index for ETS (ie exposure during childhood or at work). The authors also concluded that "When all the results are considered, and even when meta–analysis is used, the epidemiological data do not support an inference of causality or even genuinely elevated risk."

22. We consider that the meta–analysis prepared for the TMA provides a limited narrative review of the studies included, and note that appropriate sensitivity analyses were not undertaken and also that the overall assessment has been based on meta–analyses using the fixed effects model rather than the preferred random effects model. However, we agree that there is little difference between the results obtained in this paper using either model in respect of the data on smoking by the husband. We note that the results obtained for smoking by the husband [unadjusted RR = 1.19 (95% CI 1.10–1.27) and adjusted RR = 1.16 (95% CI 1.08–1.24)] and smoking by the spouse [unadjusted RR = 1.19 (95% CI 1.11–1.28) and adjusted RR = 1.17 (95% CI 1.09–1.25)] were consistent with the meta–analysis conducted by the US Environmental Protection Agency (EPA).[3] There was generally good consistency of the data when all information on spousal smoking was considered and that geographical heterogeneity may have been introduced by one particular paper from China[106] which reported an implausible protective effect of passive smoking, but the appropriate analyses to investigate this possibility were not available. The meta–analysis report identified potential sources of confounding and bias in epidemiological studies of passive smoking but the only adjustment undertaken was for misclassification bias in a supplementary report. We note that no assessment of the dose–response was undertaken in the meta–analysis and consider that the assessment of dose–response by evaluation of the statistical significance of results obtained in individual investigations was not appropriate as many of these studies had limited statistical power. We also note that the authors had not considered under–estimation bias which would attempt to adjust for the exposure of referent groups to ETS.

Meta–analysis prepared for SCOTH by Hackshaw and Wald

23.   A meta–analysis of 38 studies was undertaken using a random effects model. The reasons for excluding other studies cited in the paper submitted to SCOTH by the TMA were clearly stated. The authors noted that this meta–analysis included 25 more studies that the previous paper on ETS by the same group which was published in 1986.[107] The authors considered that the assessment of ETS exposure in childhood had not been validated and that none of the available epidemiological studies of childhood exposure reported risk of cancer stratified by whether spouse smoked or not. Regarding exposure to ETS at work, the authors noted this varied considerably between different work environments and had not been well defined and was also difficult to quantify in questionnaires. We concur with the authors decision to base their meta–analysis on spousal studies. An interim analysis based on 34 studies reported an overall risk estimate of 1.24 (95% CI 1.11–1.38).[108] In the submitted meta–analysis there were 5 cohort studies and 33 case–control studies. Odds ratios (ORs) were calculated for 30/33 of the case–control studies, the published odds ratio was used for the remaining 3 case–control studies. The authors commented that the calculated ORs were similar to the adjusted relative risk estimates in the published papers. Age–adjusted relative risk estimates were taken from the cohort studies. The majority of results reported in the meta–analysis document considered the 36 studies which presented data on non–smoking women (91% of cohort). There were 4340 lung cancer cases . Nine studies presented separate data for men (263 cases). The pooled RR from the 36 studies was 1.25 (95% CI 1.13–1.38) and was not significantly altered (ie RR = 1.24) if the data for men and for the two studies reporting men and women combined were included. Further meta–analyses using dose response data from 16 of the studies provided evidence of a dose–response based on number of cigarettes smoked per day by the spouse and number of years women lived with a spouse who smoked. The findings remained statistically significant after adjustment for misclassification bias using an estimate derived from UK data (7%), underestimation bias (due to some exposure of the reference group to ETS) and dietary confounding.

24.   This paper presents a narrative review of the methods used and the inclusion criteria, but not of the individual studies. We agree that the methods of analysis were acceptable, based on the random effects model. The overall relative risk estimate of 1.25 (95%

CI 1.13–1.38) was consistent with the result obtained by the EPA.[3] No evidence of heterogeneity was reported when one particular study (discussed in paragraph 22 above) was excluded from the analysis.[106] The results of this meta–analysis were subject to careful interpretation with appropriate meta–analysis of dose–response undertaken, adjustment for misclassification bias by current and former smokers and for potential dietary confounding. A sensitivity analysis was performed which suggested that the risk estimate would remain significant, even if a more extreme misclassification rate was assumed. One aspect of the correction for misclassification of ever smokers as non–smokers is of some concern since the data used to make the correction are from the UK. Whether these data are applicable to other, particularly non–westernised, populations is not known. However, we recognise that the best available information was used to adjust for misclassification bias.

25. The authors commented that the excess risk in non–smoking women living with men who smoked is consistent with the calculated level of cotinine (and nicotine) in these individuals compared to active smokers (ca 1%). Preliminary information from a new analysis based on data provided for the 1994 Health Survey for England suggest that the level of cotinine in adults exposed to spousal ETS is about 0.6–0.7% of the level in active smokers.[109] We consider that cotinine is a useful general indicator of recent exposure to ETS[110–114] but cannot be used to quantify accumulated doses of carcinogens attributable to passive smoking . However the risk analysis in this report based on cotinine was generally supportive of the meta–analysis of the epidemiological data. The authors also stated that the concentrations of major tobacco smoke carcinogens in the blood and urine of passive smokers were higher than in unexposed individuals which is consistent with our evaluation of these data reported in paragraph 17 above.

26. The report also comments that pathological indicators of lung cancer (examples quoted included basal cell hyperplasia and squamous cell metaplasia) were more prevalent in women living with men who smoke compared to unexposed women.[115] Overall we consider that results of this study and the most recent follow up report[116] support the view that lung tissues from non–smoking women living with smoking men were more likely to show morphological abnormalities in the bronchial epithelium and mucus glands than similar tissues from non–smoking women living with non–smoking men.

Ad–hoc European Working Group report

27 We also considered a report from an ad–hoc European Working Group. The meta–analysis was only briefly described, for example, there was no narrative explanation of the methods and the account of the criteria for inclusion of studies and evaluation of results was limited. An overall RR of 1.16 (95% CI 1.08–1.25) unadjusted and 1.08 (1.00–1.16) adjusted was reported. The authors subdivided the studies according to regional groups as follows: USA, Europe, China, HongKong and Japan, and considered that there were significant differences in the results between the groups. It is unclear whether a formal test of heterogeneity was undertaken. We concluded, on inspection of the data provided, that there was unlikely to be significant heterogeneity, but that among the studies from China there were some which showed no evidence of any effect. This may well be due to confounding risk factors such as indoor air pollution, particular to those studies. The authors reviewed the composition of ETS and presented an analysis of the components of ETS commenting on the likely exposure to genotoxic carcinogens present in ETS. However, the relevant published adduct studies regarding exposure to ETS or fresh SS reviewed in paragraph 17 above were not considered by the ad–hoc European Working Group in their report. Overall the analysis

of the epidemiological data was similar to that presented in the report commissioned for the TMA and hence the Committee agreed that this report did not add any new relevant information to the consideration of passive smoking and lung cancer.

Consideration of submitted meta–analysis reports

28. Both the submitted meta–analysis reports (prepared for the TMA and for SCOTH) document similar risk estimates that are consistent with the value reported by the EPA in 1992 of between 1.1–1.3. There were however, considerable differences in interpretation of the results. We consider that the Hackshaw and Wald meta–analysis presents a more thorough consideration of the epidemiological data. In particular this document reports a meta–analysis of dose response data and uses the best available data to adjust for dietary confounding, misclassification bias and under estimation of exposure.

Discussion and Conclusion

29. The consideration as to whether passive smoking is causally related to lung cancer starts from the standpoint that active smoking is recognised as a major cause of lung cancer. There is an approximately linear dose–response between daily consumption of cigarettes by active smokers and lung cancer risk,[4] which we consider is consistent with a lack of a threshold. Moreover active smoking is associated with elevated levels of carcinogen DNA adducts in a number of tissues including the lung and with elevated levels of protein adducts including 4–ABP and TSNA haemoglobin adducts.[88,97–102] We conclude that there are sufficient data available to show that ETS contains known genotoxic carcinogens and that exposure to ETS results in increased doses of genotoxic carcinogens to the lung with increased carcinogen–protein adducts also documented in passive smokers. A tabulated summary of the available evidence regarding passive smoking and lung cancer using the criteria established by Sir Austin Bradford–Hill is given on the next page:

Criterion	Evidence regarding passive smoking	Comments
Strength	No	Only a weak effect would be predicted from the nature of exposure. Three separate meta-analyses reviewed in this statement produced a similar overall relative risk of approximately 1.25.
Consistency	Yes	Most of the published meta-analyses considered in this report show consistent evidence of a small increase in relative risk. No heterogeneity was reported by Hackshaw and Wald when data from one Chinese study was excluded.
Specificity	Not assessed	Evidence for tumours at other sites has not been considered in this review.
Temporality	Yes	The results of retrospective studies were consistent with the few prospective studies in the meta-analyses where exposure was assessed prior to diagnosis of lung cancer.
Biological gradient	Yes	Demonstrated in meta-analyses submitted to SCOTH by Hackshaw and Wald.
Plausibility	Yes	Evidence of exposure of the lung to genotoxic carcinogens present in ETS, data from published reports of increased carcinogen-protein adducts in passive smokers and the linear nature of the dose response for lung cancer in active smokers, indicate it is plausible that ETS induce lung cancer.
Coherence	Yes	The available information on passive smoking (epidemiological, biological monitoring studies for exposure using cotinine, and evidence from protein adduct investigations) are coherent.
Experiment	Limited	Possible only in animals. Limited evidence that SS which predominantly forms ETS is carcinogenic in animals. Sufficient evidence that MS is carcinogenic in animals No adequate study with ETS.
Analogy	Yes	An association between passive smoking and lung cancer is consistent with the known casual association for active smoking and lung cancer.

30. Taking all the supporting data into consideration we conclude that there is evidence to satisfy six of the nine criteria and limited evidence for one of the remaining criteria (experiment) established by Bradford–Hill to assess the causality of an exposure–disease association. We would not anticipate the strength criteria to be fulfilled, given the low level of exposure, and there are no data with which to assess specificity. In fulfilling the other criteria, we conclude that passive smoking in non–smokers exposed over a substantial part of their life is associated with a 10–30% increase in the risk of lung cancer which could account for several hundred lung cancer deaths per annum in the UK.

31. Thus in summary our conclusions regarding passive smoking and lung cancer are;

Composition /Exposure

(i) MS, SS and ETS contain the same carcinogens and although there will be quantitative differences in composition between different types of smoke, it is likely that the exposure of active and passive smokers to carcinogens will be qualitatively similar **(Paragraph 6)**. We consider that there are sufficient data to conclude that passive smoking results in an increased dose of genotoxic carcinogens to the respiratory tract and including the alveolar region of the lung. **(paragraph 10)**

Biological properties

(ii) Exposure to mutagenic particles present in ETS occurs under a wide range of field conditions and is likely to occur under all conditions where passive smoking occurs. **(Paragraph 12)**

(iii) Whole MS and its condensate and SS condensates are carcinogenic in animals which suggests that ETS will also be carcinogenic to animals. However we note that there are no appropriate life–time bioassays using ETS available. **(Paragraph 13)**

(iv) Exposure to ETS over a wide range of exposure levels, including those normally encountered in homes, at work and in public places can lead to the inhalation and delivery of genotoxic carcinogens to all parts of the respiratory tract. Furthermore such compounds will be in contact with cells capable of activation to produce the proximate carcinogens. This gives rise to concern regarding increased carcinogenic risk of lung cancer, although it is not possible to make any quantitative estimate of risk from these particular data. The COC advice on genotoxic carcinogens is to make the prudent assumption that any exposure may be associated with some increased health detriment, in this case a risk of lung cancer. **(Paragraph 18)**

Submitted meta–analysis reports

(v) Both the submitted meta–analysis reports (prepared for TMA and for SCOTH) document similar risk estimates that are consistent with the value reported by the EPA in 1992 of between 1.1–1.3. However there are considerable differences in interpretation of the results. We are of the view that the paper prepared for SCOTH by Hackshaw and Wald presents a more thorough consideration of the epidemiological data. In particular this document reports a meta–analysis of dose response data and uses the best available data to adjust for dietary confounding, misclassification bias and under estimation of exposure. **(Paragraph 28)**

Overall conclusion

(vi) Taking all the supporting data into consideration we conclude that passive smoking in non–smokers exposed over a substantial part of their life is associated with a 10–30% increase in the risk of lung cancer which could account for several hundred lung cancer deaths per annum in the UK. **(Paragraph 30)**

References

1. *Environmental tobacco smoke and lung cancer: an evaluation of the risk: report of a European working group.* Trondheim: Trondheim European Working Party, 1996. Chairman: JR Idle.

2. Department of Health. *The health of the nation: smoke–free for health: an action plan to achieve the health of the nation targets.* London: Department of Health, 1994; 59.

3. EPA. *Respiratory health effects of passive smoking: lung cancers and other disorders: US Environmental Protection Agency.* Washington: Office of Air and Radiation, 1992. (EPA/600/6–90/006F).

4. World Health Organisation. International agency for research on cancer: IARC monographs on the evaluation of the carcinogenic risk of chemicals to humans: Tobacco smoking. Pub. IARC, Lyons 1986: 421. (vol 38)

5. National Resesearch Council. *Environmental tobacco smoke: measuring exposures and assessing health effects: Committee on Passive Smoking Board on Environmental Studies and Toxicology.* Washington DC: National Academy Press, 1986.

6. *Independent Scientific Committee on Smoking and Health: fourth report.* London: HMSO, 1988.

7. Armitage A K, Ashford J R, Gorrod J W, Sullivan F M. Environmental tobacco smoke: is it really a carcinogen. *Medical Science Research* 1997; **25**: 3–7.

8. Lee P N. Passive smoking and lung cancer association: a result of bias? *Human Toxicol* 1987; **6**: 78–85.

9. Fleiss J L, Gross A J. Meta–analysis in epidemiology, with special reference to studies of the association between exposure to environmental tobacco smoke and lung cancer: a critique. *J Clin Epidemiol* 1991; **44**: 127–139.

10. Tobacco Manufacturers Association. *A review of the epidemiology of ETS and lung cancer.* Unpublished report submitted to SCOTH, 1996.

11. Nilsson R. Review of environmental tobacco smoke and lung cancer: a reappraisal. *Ecotoxicol Environ Safety* 1996; **34**: 2–17.

12. Department of Health. *Report on health and social subjects: guidelines for the evaluation of chemicals for carcinogenicity: Committee on Carcinogenicity of Chemicals in Food, Consumer Products and the Environment.* London: HMSO, 1991; 80. (vol 42).

13. Bradford–Hill A. The environment and disease: association or causation? *Proceedings of the Royal Society of Medicine* 1965; **58**: 295–300.

14. World Health Organisation. Tomatis L, ed. *Cancer: causes occurrence and control.* Lyon: International Agency for Research on Cancer, 1990; 352. (IARC Scientific publication no 100)

15. Guerin M R, Jenkins R A, Tomkins B A. *The chemistry of environmental tobacco smoke: composition and measurement.* Michigan: Lewis, 1992.

16. Guerin M R. Formation and physical nature of sidestream smoke. In: O'neill I K, Brunnemann K D, Bodet B, Hoffmann D, eds. *Environmental carcinogens methods of analysis and exposure measurement.* Lyon: International Agency for Research on Cancer, 1987; 11–24. (Passive smoking; vol 9). (IARC Scientific publication no 81).

17. McAughey J. *Environmental tobacco smoke: a critical review of the dosimetry.* AEA Technology plc, Harwell. Unpublished report produced for the Tobacco Manufacturer's Association, 1997.

18. Baker R R, Procter C J. The origins and properties of environmental tobacco smoke. *Environ Intern* 1990; **16**: 231–45.

19. Eatough D J, Hansen L D, Lewis E A. The chemical characterisation of environmental tobacco smoke. *Environ Technol* 1990; **11**: 1071–85.

20. Gori G B, Mantel N. Mainstream and environmental tobacco smoke. *Regul Toxicol Pharmacol* 1991; **18**: 88–105.

21. Rawbone R R, Burns W, Haslett G. The aging of sidestream tobacco components in ambient environments. *Indoor Air Quality* 1990: 55–61.

22. Brunnemann K D, Yu L, Hoffmann D. Assessment of carcinogenic volatile nitrosamines in tobacco and in mainstream and sidestream smoke from cigarettes. *Cancer Res* 1977; **37**: 3218–22.

23. Hoffmann D, Adams J D, Brunnemann K D, Hecht S S. Assessment of tobacco–specific N–nitrosamines in tobacco products. *Cancer Res* 1979; **39**: 2505–9.

24. Adams J D, O'Mara–Adams K J, Hoffmann D. Toxic and carcinogenic agents in undiluted mainstream smoke and sidestream smoke of different types of cigarettes. *Carcinogenesis* 1987; **8**: 729–31.

25. Lofroth G. Environmental tobacco smoke: overview of chemical composition and genotoxic components. *Mutat Res* 1989; **222**: 73–80.

26. Department of Health. *In confidence report on determination of tobacco specific nitrosamines in mainstream and sidestream smoke of cigarettes.* Teddington: Unpublished report by the Laboratory of the Government Chemist, 1994.

27.   Chortyk O, Schlotzhauer W S. The contribution of low tar cigarettes to environmental tobacco smoke. *J Anal Toxicol* 1989; **13**: 129–34.

28.   Patrianakos C, Hoffmann D. Chemical studies on tobacco smoke LXIV: on the analysis of aromatic amines in cigarette smoke. *J Anal Toxicol* 1979; **3**: 150–4.

29.   Sterling T D, Mueller B. Concentrations of nicotine RSP, CO and CO_2 in non–smoking areas of offices ventilated by air recirculated from smoking designated areas. *American Industrial Hygiene Association J* 1988; **49**: 423–6.

30.   Turner S, Cyr L, Gross A J. The measurement of environmental tobacco smoke in 585 offices. *Environ Intern* 1992; **18**: 19–28.

31.   Oldaker G B, Taylor W D, Parish K B. Investigations of ventilation, smoking activity, and indoor air quality at four large office buildings. In: *Proceedings of indoor air quality 1993*. ASHRE, 1992; 248–57.

32.   Hedge A, Erickson W A, Rubin G. The effects of alternative smoking policies on indoor air quality in 27 office buildings. *Ann Occup Hyg* 1994; **38**: 265–78.

33.   Scherer G, Conze C, Tricker A R, Adlkofer F. Uptake of tobacco smoke constituents on exposure to environmental tobacco smoke (ETS). *Clin Investig* 1992; **70**: 352–67.

34.   Phillips K, Howard D A, Browne D, Lewsley J M. Assessment of personal exposures to environmental tobacco smoke in British non–smokers. *Environ Intern* 1994; **20**: 693–712.

35.   Jenkins R A. Determination of personal exposure of non–smokers to environmental tobacco smoke in the United States. *Lung Cancer* 1996; **14(suppl)**: S195–S213.

36.   Phillips K et al. Assessment of air quality in Stockholm by personal monitoring of non–smokers for respirable suspended particles and environmental tobacco smoke. *Scand J Work Environ Health* 1996; **22(suppl 1)**: 1–24.

37.   Holocomb L C. Indoor air quality and environmental tobacco smoke: concentration and exposure. *Environ Intern* 1993; **19**: 9–40.

38.   Husgafvel–Pursiainen K, Sorsa M, Moller M, Benestad C. Genotoxicity and polynuclear aromatic hydrocarbon analysis of environmental tobacco smoke samples from restaurants. *Mutagenesis* 1986; **1**: 287–92.

39.   Salomaa S, Tuominen J, Skytta E. Genotoxicity and PAC analysis of particulate and vapour phases of environmental tobacco smoke. *Mutat Res* 1988; **204**: 173–83.

40.   Brunnemann K D, Cox J E, Hoffmann D. Analysis of tobacco–specific N–nitrosamines in indoor air. *Carcinogenesis* 1992; **13**: 2415–18.

41.   Wallace L A, Pellizzari. Personal air exposures and breath concentrations of benzene and other volatile hydrocarbons for smokers and non–smokers. *Toxicol Lett* 1986; **35**: 113–16.

42.   Heavner D L, Morgan W T, Ogden M W. Determination of volatile organic compounds and ETS apportionment in 49 homes. *Environ Intern* 1995; **21**: 3–21.

43.   Brown V, Crump D R. Volatile organic compounds. In: Berry RW, ed. *Indoor air quality in homes: part 1: the building research establishment indoor environment study.*
London: Construction Research Communications, 1996; 38–62.

44.   Hoffmann D, Adams J D, Brunnemann. A critical look at N–nitrosamines in environmental tobacco smoke. *Toxicol Lett* 1987; **35**: 1–8.

45.   Hecht S S, Carmella S G, Murphy S E, Akerkar S, Brunnemann K D, Hoffmann D. A
tobacco–specific lung carcinogen in the urine of men exposed to cigarette smoke. *N
Engl J Med* 1993; **329**: 1543–6.

46.   Repace J L. Indoor concentrations of environmental tobacco smoke: models dealing
with effects of ventilation and room size. In: O'neill I K, Brunnemann K D, Bodet B,
Hoffmann D, eds. *Environmental carcinogens methods of analysis and exposure measurement: passive smoking.* Lyon: International Agency of Research on Cancer, 1987;
25–42. (IARC Scientific publication no 81).

47.   Repace J L, Lowrey A H. Indoor air pollution, tobacco smoke and public health.
Science 1980; **208**: 464–72.

48.   Hammond S K, Leaderer B P, Roche A C, Schenker M. Collection and analysis of nicotine as a marker for environmental tobacco smoke. *Atmospheric Environ* 1987; **21**:
457–62.

49.   Hiller F C, McCusker K T, Mazumder M K, Wilson J D, Bone R C. Deposition of sidestream cigarette smoke in the human respiratory tract. *Am Rev Respiratory Disease* 1982;
125: 406–8.

50.   Hinds W, First M W, Huber G L, Shea J W. A method for measuring respiratory deposition of cigarette smoke during smoking. *Am Ind Hyg Assoc J* 1983; **44**: 113–18.

51.   Department of Health. *Committee on the Medical Effects of Air Pollutants: non biological particles and health.* London: HMSO, 1995.

52.   Oberdorster G, Pott F. Extrapolation from rat studies with environmental tobacco smoke
(ETS) to human: comparison of particle mass deposition and of clearance behaviour of
ETS compounds. *Toxicol Lett* 1987; **35**: 107–12.

53.   Grover P L. K–region epoxides of polycyclic hydrocarbons: formation and further
metabolism of benz(a)anthracene 5,6: oxide by human lung preparations. *FEBS Lett*
1973; **34**: 63–8.

54.   Castonguay A, Stoner G D, Schut H A J, Hecht S S. Metabolism of tobacco specific
N–nitrosamines by cultured human tissues: proceedings of the National Academy of
Sciences 1983; **80**: 6694–7.

55.   van Houdt J J, Jongen V M F, Alink G M, Boleij J S M. Mutagenic activity of airborne
particles inside and outside homes. *Environ Mutagenesis* 1984; **6**: 861–9.

56.   Löfroth G, Lazaridis G. Environmental tobacco smoke: comparative characterisation by
mutagenicity assays of sidestream and mainstream cigarette smoke. *Environ
Mutagenesis* 1986; **8**: 693–704.

57.   Husgafvel–Pursiainen K, Sorsa M, M?ller M, Benestad C. Genotoxicity and polynuclear aromatic hydrocarbon analysis of environmental tobacco smoke samples from restaurants. *Mutagenesis* 1986; **1**: 287–92.

58.   Ling P I, Löfroth G, Lewtas J. Mutagenic determination of passive smoking. *Toxicol Lett* 1987; **35**: 147–51.

59.   Claxton L D, Morin R S, Hughes T J, Lewtas J. A genotoxic assessment of environmental tobacco smoke using bacterial bioassays. *Mutat Res* 1989; **222**: 81–99.

60.   Löfroth G, Stensman C, Brandhorst–Satzkorn M. Indoor sources of mutagenic aerosol particulate matter: smoking, cooking and incense burning. *Mutat Res* 1991; **261**: 21–8.

61.   Kado N Y, McCurdy S A, Tesluk S J, et al. Measuring personal exposure to airborne mutagens and nicotine in environmental tobacco smoke. *Mutat Res* 1991; **261**: 75–82.

62.   Chen C, Lee H. Genotoxicity and DNA adduct formation of incense smoke condensates: comparison with environmental tobacco smoke condensates. *Mutat Res* 1996; **367**: 105–14.

63.   Mohtashamipur E, Norpoth K, Straeter H. Clastogenic effect of passive smoking on bone marrow polychromatic erythrocytes of NMRI mice. *Toxicol Lett* 1987; **35**: 153–6.

64.   Lee C K, Brown B G. Fourteen day inhalation study in rats using aged diluted sidestream smoke from a reference cigarette: II DNA adducts and alveolar macrophage cytogenetics. *Fundam Appl Toxicol* 1992; **19**: 141–6.

65.   Lee C K, Brown B D. Ninety–day inhalation study in rats, using aged and diluted sidestream smoke from a reference cigarette: DNA adducts and alveolar macrophage cytogenetics. *Fundam Appl Toxicol* 1993; **20**: 393–401.

66.   TakenawaJ, Kaneko Y, Okumura K, Nakayama H, Fujita J, Yoshida O. Urinary excretion of mutagens and covalent DNA damage induced in the bladder and kidney after passive smoking in rats. *Urology Res* 1994; **22**: 93–7.

67.   Grimmer G, Brune H, Dettbarn G, Naujack K W, Mohr U, Wenzel–Hartung R. Contribution of polycyclic aromatic compounds to the carcinogenicity of sidestream smoke of cigarettes evaluated by implantation into the lungs of rats. *Cancer Lett* 1988; **43**: 173–7.

68.   Mohtashamipur E, Mohtashamipur, A, Germann P G, Ernst H, Norpoth K, Mohr U. Comparative carcinogenicity of cigarette mainstream and sidestream smoke condensates on the mouse skin. *J Cancer Res Clin Oncol* 1990; **116**: 604–8.

69.   Wynder E L, Hoffmann D. Biological tests for tumorigenic and cilia–toxic activity. In: *Tobacco and tobacco smoke: studies in experimental carcinogenesis*. New York: Academic Press, 1967; 183–4.

70.   Witschi H, Espiritu I, Peake J L, Wu K, Maronpot R R, Pinkerton K E. The carcinogenicity of environmental tobacco smoke. *Carcinogenesis* 1997; **18**: 575–86.

71.   Witschi H, Oreffo V I, Pinkerton K E. Six–month exposure of strain A/J mice to ciga-rette sidestream smoke: cell kinetics and lung tumour data. *Fundam Appl Toxicol* 1995; **26**: 32–40.

72.   Coggins R E, Ayres P H, Mosberg A T, Ogden M W, Sagartz J W, Hayes A W. Fourteen–day inhalation study in rats, using aged and diluted sidestream smoke from a reference cigarette: I: inhalation toxicology and histopathology. *Fundam Appl Toxicol* 1992; **19**: 133–40.

73.   Coggins C R E, Ayres P H, Mosberg A T, Sagartz J W, Hayes A W. Subchronic inhala-tion study in rats using aged and diluted sidestream smoke from a reference cigarette. *Inhalation Toxicology* 1993; **5**: 77–96.

74.   Sorsa M, Husgafvel–Pursiainen K, Järventaus H, Koskimies, K, Salo H, Vainio H. Cytogenetic effects of tobacco smoke exposure among involuntary smokers. *Mutat Res* 1989; **222**: 111–16.

75.   Crawford F G. Biomarkers and environmental tobacco smoke in preschool children and their mothers. *J Natl Cancer Inst* 1994; 86: 1398–1402.

76.   Maclure M, Katz R B, Bryant M S, Skipper P L, Tannenbaum S R. Elevated blood levels of carcinogens in passive smokers. *Am J Public Health* 1989; **79**: 1381–4.

77.   Hammond S K, Coghlin J, Gann P H et al. Relationship between environmental tobac-co smoke exposure in carcinogen–haemoglobin adduct levels in nonsmokers. *J Natl Cancer Inst* 1993; **85:** 474–7.

78.   Bos R P, Theuws J L G, Henderson P T H. Excretion of mutagens in human urine after passive smoking. *Cancer Lett* 1983; **19**: 85–90.

79.   Sorsa M, Einisto P. Passive and active exposure to cigarette smoke in a smoking exper-iment. *J Toxicol Environ Health* 1985; **16:** 523–34.

80.   Husgafvel–Pursiainen K, Sorsa M, Engström, Einisto P. Passive smoking at work: bio-chemical and biological measures to exposure to environmental tobacco smoke. *Int Arch Occup Environ Health* 1987; **59**: 337–45.

81.   Perera F P, Santella R M. DNA adducts, protein adducts, and sister chromatidexchange in cigarette smokers and nonsmokers. *J Natl Cancer Inst* 1987; **79**: 449–56.

82.   Scherer G, Westphal K, Biber A, Koepfner I, Adlkofer F. Urinary mutagenicity after con-trolled exposure to environmental tobacco smoke (ETS). *Toxicol Lett* 1987; **35**: 135–40.

83.   Mohtashamipur E, Müller G, Norpoth K, Endrikat M, Stücker W. Urinary excretion of mutagens in passive smokers. *Toxicol Lett* 1987; **35**: 141–6.

84.   Gorgels W J M J, van Poppel G, Jarvis M J, Stenhuis W, Kok F J. Passive smoking and sister–chromatid exchanges in lymphocytes. *Mutat Res* 1992; **279**: 223–38.

85.   Autrup H, Vestergaar A B, Okkels H. Transplacental transfer of environmental geno-toxins: polycyclic aromatic hydrocarbon–albumin in non–smoking women, and the effect of maternal GSTM1 genotype. *Carcinogenesis* 1995; **16**: 1305–9.

86. Sasson I M, Coleman D T, LaVoie E J, Hoffmann D, Wynder E L. Mutagens in human urine: effects of cigarette smoking and diet. *Mutat Res* 1985; **158**: 149–57.

87. Bartsch H, Caporaso N. Carcinogen haemoglobin adducts, urinary mutagenicity, and metabolic phenotype in active and passive cigarette smokers. *J Natl Cancer Inst* 1990; **82**: 1826–31.

88. Phillips D H, Schoket B, Hewer A, Bailey E, Kostic S, Vincze I. Influence of cigarette smoking on levels of DNA adducts in human bronchial epithelium and white blood cells. *Int J Cancer* 1990; **46**: 569–75.

89. van Schooten F J. Polycyclic aromatic hydrocarbon–DNA adducts in white blood cells from lung cancer patients: no correlation with adduct levels in lung. *Carcinogenesis* 1992; **13**: 987–93.

90. Jahnke G D, Thompson C L, Walker M P, Gallagher J E, Lucier G W, DiAugustine R. Multiple DNA adducts in lymphocytes of smokers and nonsmokers determined by ^{32}P–postlabelling analysis. *Carcinogenesis* 1990; **11**: 205–11.

91. van Maanen J M S, Maas L M, Hageman G, Kleinjans J C S, van Agen B. DNA adduct and mutation analysis in white blood cells of smokers and nonsmokers. *Environ Mol Mutagen* 1994; **24**: 46–50.

92. Farmer P. Biomonitoring and molecular dosimetry of genotoxic carcinogens. In: DeMatteis F, Smith LL, eds. *Molecular and cellular mechanisms of toxicity*. London: CRC Press, 1995; 101–23.

93. Perera F P. The significance of DNA and protein adducts in human biomonitoring studies. *Mutat Res* 1988; **205**: 255–269.

94. Skipper P L, Tannenbaum S R. Protein adducts in the molecular dosimetry of chemical carcinogens. *Carcinogenesis* 1990; **11**: 507–18.

95. Reasor M J. Relationship between environmental tobaccos smoke exposure and carcinogen–haemoglobin adduct levels in nonsmokers. *J Natl Cancer Inst* 1993; **85:** 1693–4.

96. Hammond S K, Coghlin J, Gann P H, Skipper P L, Tannenbaum S R. Response to Reasor M J. *J Natl Cancer Inst* 1993; **85**: 1694–6.

97. Carmella S G. Mass spectrometric analysis of tobacco–specific nitrosamine haemoglobin adducts in snuff dippers, smokers and nonsmokers. *Cancer Res* 1990; **50**: 5438–45.

98. Bryant M S, Skipper P L, Tannenbaum S R, Maclure M. Haemoglobin adducts of 4–aminobiphenyl in smokers and nonsmokers. *Cancer Res* 1987; **47**: 602–8.

99. Randerath E, Miller R H, Mittal D, Avitts T A, Dunsford H A, Randerath K. Covalent DNA damage in tissues of cigarette smokers as determined by ^{32}P–postlabelling assay. *J Natl Cancer Inst* 1989; **81**: 341–7.

100. Savela K, Hemminki K. DNA adducts in lymphocytes and granulocytes of smokers and nonsmokers detected by the ^{32}P–postlabelling assay. *Carcinogenesis* 1991; **12**: 503–8.

101.   Lewtas J. Comparison of DNA Adducts from exposure to complex mixtures in various human tissues and experimental systems. *Environ Health Perspect* 1993; **99**: 89–97.

102.   Phillips D H. DNA adducts in human tissues: biomarkers of exposure to carcinogens in tobacco smoke. *Environ Health Perspect* 1996; **104(suppl 3)**: 453–8.

103.   Kawachi I, Colditz G A. Invited commentary: confounding, measurement error and publication bias in studies of passive smoking. *Am J Epidemiol* 1996; **144**: 909–15.

104.   Dockery D W, Trichopoulos D. Risk of lung cancer from environmental exposures to tobacco smoke. *Cancer Causes Control* 1997; **8:** 333–45.

105.   Peto J. Meta–analysis of epidemiological studies of carcinogenesis. In: Vainio H, Magee P N, McGregor D B, McMichael A J, eds. *Mechanisms of carcinogenesis in risk identification*. Lyon: International Agency for Research on Cancer, 1992; 571–7.

106.   Wu–Williams A H. Lung cancer among women in north–east China. *Br J Cancer* 1990; **62**: 982–7.

107.   Wald N J, Nanchahal K, Thompson S G, Cuckle H S. Does breathing other people's tobacco smoke cause lung cancer? *BMJ* 1986; **293**: 1217–22.

108.   Law M R, Hackshaw A K. Environmental tobacco smoke. *Br Med Bull* 1996; **52**: 22–34.

109.   Jarvis M. Imperial Cancer Research Fund, Health Behaviour Unit, University College London. Personal communication to COC secretariat. 1997.

110.   Jarvis M J, McNeill A. Factors determining exposure to passive smoking in young adults living at home: quantitative analysis using saliva cotinine concentrations. *Int J Epidemiol* 1991; **20**: 126–31.

111.   Riboli E. Exposure of nonsmoking women to environmental tobacco smoke: a 10 country collaborative study. *Cancer Causes Control* 1990; **1**: 243–52.

112.   Matsukura S. Effects of environmental tobacco smoke on urinary cotinine excretion in nonsmokers: evidence for passive smoking. *N Engl J Med* 1984; **311**: 828–32.

113.   Blot W J, Fraumeni J F. Passive smoking and lung cancer. *J Natl Cancer Inst* 1986; **77**: 993–1000.

114.   Benowitz N L. Cotinine as a biomarker of environmental tobacco smoke exposure. *Epidemiol Rev* 1996; **18**: 188–204.

115.   Trichopolous D. Active and passive smoking and pathological indicators of lung cancer risk in an autopsy study. *JAMA* 1992; **268**: 1697–1701.

116.   Agapitos E. Epithelial, possibly precancerous, lesions of the lung in relation to smoking, passive smoking, and socio–demographic variables. *Scand J Soc Med* 1996; **24**: 259–63.

ANNEX I

EXECUTIVE SUMMARY

Systematic Quantitative Review of the Effect of Environmental Tobacco Smoke Exposure on Respiratory Health in Children

Derek G Cook
David P Strachan
H Ross Anderson
Department of Public Health Science, St George's Hospital Medical School, London SW17 ORE

Background

During the last two decades, many epidemiological studies have reported on the association between parental smoking and respiratory diseases in childhood. These were considered in both the US Surgeon General's 1986 report and the Environmental Protection Agency Report (1993). However these and most other reviews have been neither systematic nor meta–analytic in their approach. Moreover, a large number of publications have occurred since the completion of the EPA report.

Our aim was to systematically review the health effects of Environmental Tobacco Smoke (ETS) in children's respiratory health and where possible to produce meta–analytic estimates of the relative risks. In carrying out the review we were particularly concerned to consider the importance of residual confounding from other environmental factors as a possible explanation for any differences found and to assess the relative importance of exposure at different ages. We also distinguished wherever possible between the effects of smoking by different household members and between pre- and post-natal exposure.

Report Structure

Summary of the review process, findings and conclusions (this document)
Separate chapters on:

Sudden Infant Death Syndrome

Lower Respiratory Tract Illness in pre–school children

Prevalence of asthma & respiratory symptoms in schoolchildren

Incidence, severity and prognosis of asthma

Bronchial Hyper–Reactivity

Allergic sensitisation

Ear disease and adenotonsillectomy

Review Process

Published papers, letters and review articles were selected by an electronic search of the Embase and Medline databases, using the search strategy described in the Appendix. briefly all passive smoking references were selected by the MESH heading *Tobacco smoke pollution* and/or relevant text–words in the title, keywords or abstract. Papers were then restricted to children by selecting all papers classified as containing data on neonates to 18 years and/or by relevant text–words in the title or abstract. Embase searches were entirely based on text–word searches. This search, completed in March 1996, yielded 3365 references which were downloaded into Reference Manager. After further electronic text–word searching (see appendix) and review of the on–line abstracts, 605 articles were identified as relevant to the broader overview. 385 (64%) of these had been published during 1990–96, the remainder during 1972–89. The number of studies included under each heading are summarised in table 1.

Main Findings (See Table 2 for overall summary of odds ratios for different outcomes)

Sudden Infant Death Syndrome

Maternal smoking during pregnancy was clearly associated with a risk of sudden infant death, with all 35 studies showing a relative risk greater than 1 which was statistically significant in all but 2 studies. The pooled odds ratio for studies not adjusting for confounding variables was 2.49 (95% CI 2.28–2.72). In studies which adjusted for potential confounding variables the pooled odds ratio was 2.08 (95% CI 1.96–2.21). While it is difficult to distinguish the independent effects of pre- and post-natal smoking by the mother, those studies which examined the issue found evidence of a post-natal effect. Such a conclusion is strengthened by evidence from 3 studies reporting on risk of paternal smoking where the mother was a non–smoker. Two reported significant effects, 1 no effect with a pooled odds ratio of 1.63 (95% CI 1.26–2.11).

Lower Respiratory Illness in infancy and early childhood

The pooled odds ratio for either parent smoking across all studies was 1.48 (95% CI 1.40 to 1.57) and was consistent across different study types: 1.45 (95% CI 1.34 to 1.57) for community based studies of lower respiratory illness, bronchitis and/or pneumonia; 1.54 (95% CI 1.30–1.81) for community studies of wheezing illness; 1.45 (95% CI 1.27–1.66) for studies of hospitalisation for lower respiratory illness, bronchitis, bronchiolitis or pneumonia. The associations were robust to adjustment for confounding factors, and showed evidence of dose response where this was investigated. Importantly, there was a significantly elevated risk of early chest illness associated with smoking by other household members in families where the mother did not smoke (relative odds 1.29, 95% CI 1.19–1.41). There was insufficient evidence to evaluate the independent contribution of pre- and post-natal maternal smoking.

Prevalence of Asthma and Respiratory Symptoms in School Children

The pooled odds ratios for either parent smoking were 1.17 (95% CI 1.10–1.25) for asthma; 1.24 (95% CI 1.19-1.30) for wheeze; 1.33 (95% CI 1.27–1.39) for cough; 1.33 (95% CI 1.14–1.55) for phlegm; and 1.31 (95% CI 1.14–1.50) for breathlessness. Adjustment for confounding had little effect on these estimates. Evidence of heterogeneity between studies appeared largely explicable in terms of publication bias with a superfluity of small studies with large odd ratios. However, excluding these had little effect on the pooled odds ratios. There was clear evidence that maternal smoking had a greater effect than that of paternal smoking for all conditions, though there was a significantly increased risk of each symptom associated with smoking by the father only.

For all symptoms, children exposed to two parents smoking were at greater risk, the pooled odds ratios compared to children on non–smoking parents being 1.52 (95% CI 1.34–1.72) for asthma, 1.40 (95% CI 1.29–1.51) for wheeze and 1.61 (95% CI 1.50–1.73) for cough.

Incidence, severity and prognosis of asthma

Case control studies looking at ETS and asthma prevalence provided a slightly greater odds ratio for either parent smoking than the cross–sectional surveys: 1.35 (95% CI 1.19–1.54). In longitudinal studies, maternal smoking was associated with an increased incidence of wheezing illness up to age 6 (pooled odds ratio 1.31, 95% CI 1.22–1.41) but less strongly thereafter (1.13, 95% CI 1.04–1.22). The long term prognosis of early wheezing illness was better if the mother smoked, reflecting the fact that children of smoking parents are more likely to develop mild wheezing illness at younger ages. Such an interpretation is supported by 3 studies that suggest that parental smoking is more strongly associated with wheezing amongst non–atopic children. The effect of ETS exposure on asthmatics is not however benign; indicators of disease severity, attack frequency, medication use and life–threatening bronchospasm were in general positively related to household smoking, but could not be combined in a quantitative meta–analysis.

We thus face a contradiction. Longitudinal studies demonstrate that maternal smoking is associated with an increased incidence of wheezing illness, particularly at younger ages. This excess incidence of early wheezing illness appears to be largely non–atopic "wheezy bronchitis" and to run a relatively benign course. However, amongst children with established asthma, parental smoking is associated with more severe disease. We believe that this paradox is explained by viewing ETS as a trigger of wheezing attacks (probably acting in conjunction with infection), rather than as a cause of the underlying asthmatic tendency. Our interpretation is supported by the lack of a positive association between ETS and atopic sensitisation (see below). However, the true test of the hypothesis lies in whether long term measures of asthmatic tendency such as bronchial hyper–responsiveness are associated with ETS exposure.

Bronchial hyper–reactivity (BHR)

We were able to extract effect measures from 8 studies in the form of relative odds of measured bronchial hyper–reactivity for ETS exposed children compared to non–exposed children. There was no evidence of heterogeneity between studies and no single study dominates. The pooled estimate of the relative odds was 1.28 (95% CI, 1.08 to 1.52). For 6 studies not providing odds ratios none found statistically significant effects. A further 4 studies were identified as having collected data but not published. The studies included in the meta–analysis covered 4976 children, those reporting non–significant results but not odds ratios covered 3714 children and the unpublished studies covered 4793 children.

We conclude that a clear effect of ETS exposure on BHR in the general population has not been established. While the meta–analysis suggests a small, but real, increase in BHR in school aged children, it seems likely that this estimate is biased upwards due to publication bias. In contrast limited evidence from 4 studies suggests greater variation in peak flow in children of smoking parents. Such a finding would be in keeping with acute effects of ETS exposure on airflow rather than chronic effects on BHR.

Ear Disease and Adentonsillectomy

Evidence for middle ear disease was remarkably consistent, with pooled odds ratios if either parent smoked of 1.41 (95% CI 1.19–1.65) for recurrent otitis media, 1.38 (95% CI 1.23–1.55) for middle ear effusion, and 1.21 (95% CI 0.95–1.53) for out–patient or inpatient referral for glue ear.

These associations were robust to adjustment for confounding factors and are likely to be causal. Few studies have assessed dose response. Large French and British Studies were inconsistent regarding the association between parental smoking and tonsillectomy.

Allergic Sensitisation

No consistent association were found in neonates or older children between parental smoking and total serum IgE concentration, allergic rhinitis or eczema. Some evidence of a weak inverse association was found with skin prick sensitivity with a pooled odds ratio of 0.86 (95% CI 0.77–0.97) for current passive smoke exposure and 0.94 (95% CI 0.79–1.13) for perinatal exposure. The combined odds ratio was 0.88 (95% CI 0.88–0.98. However, significant and unexplained heterogeneity of odds ratios between studies suggest the need for cautious interpretation, particularly of the confidence intervals.

Conclusions

- The relationships between parental smoking and sudden infant death and acute lower respiratory illness in infancy are almost certainly causal.

  The elevated risks associated with smoking by other household members provide good evidence that postnatal exposure from both mother and father are important.

  Because pre–natal smoking is almost invariably associated with post–natal smoking, the role of pre–natal maternal smoking will be difficult to resolve using epidemiological studies.

- There is convincing evidence that parental smoking is associated with increased prevalence of asthma and respiratory symptoms in school children.

  Among children with established asthma, parental smoking is associated with more severe disease.

  Parental smoking probably acts, alone or in combination with infection, as a trigger of wheezing attacks rather than as a cause of the underlying asthmatic tendency. ETS exposure is not consistently related to allergic sensitisation and the case for a relationship with BHR has not been established.

- It seems likely that parental smoking causes both acute and chronic middle ear disease in children. The evidence regarding tonsillectomy is inconsistent.

- Reducing parental smoking would result in important reductions in respiratory morbidity and mortality in infants and children.

Output

Thorax have agreed to publish our systematic reviews as a peer reviewed series. A series editor has been appointed and it planned that the first papers will appear in the latter half of 1997. Reviews will be updated with 1996 references prior to publication. This may results in some changes to the pooled odds ratios presented in table 2.

Table 1 Number of Papers selected for the review process

Outcome	Potentially relevant after brief review of abstracts	Included in review	Additional references identified	Total in review
SIDS	67	30	10	40
Ears & Tonsils	51	37	5	42
Allergy	172	30	2	32
Spirometry	199	30–40		30–40
Bronchial hyper–reactivity	73	27	1	28
LRI in infancy	78	47	0	47
Respiratory symptoms in schoolchildren	85	43	3	46
Asthma incidence, severity & prognosis	62	52	2	54
Total	605*			
*some papers appear under several headings				

TABLE 2: Summary of Effects of ETS on the Respiratory Health of Children

Outcome	Age (Years)	Either parent OR (95% CI)	[n]	Mother OR (95% CI)	[n]	Father only OR (95% CI)	[n]	Both Parents OR (95% CI)	[n]
SIDS				2.08 (1.96–2.21)	[19]	1.63 (1.26–2.11)	[3]		
Acute otitis media		Range 1.0–1.5	[9]						
Recurrent otitis media		1.41 (1.19–1.65)	[7]						
Middle ear effusion		1.38 (1.23–1.55)	[4]						
Referral for glue ear		1.21 (0.95–1.53)	[7]						
Lower respiratory Illness	0–2	1.48 (1.40–1.57)	[26]	1.64 (1.54–1.73)	[25]	1.29 (1.19–1.41)	[16]		
Wheeze prevalence	5–16	1.24 (1.19–1.30)	[25]	1.27 (1.18–1.36)	[16]	1.13 (1.05–1.21)	[10]	1.40 (1.29–1.51)	[10]
Cough prevalence	5–16	1.33 (1.27–1.39)	[25]	1.38 (1.26–1.51)	[12]	1.21 (1.11–1.31)	[9]	1.61 (1.50–1.73)	[15]
Phlegm prevalence	5–16	1.33 (1.14–1.55)	[5]						
Breathlessness	5–16	1.31 (1.14–1.50)	[6]						
Asthma prevalence x–s	5–16	1.17 (1.10–1.25)	[14]	1.37 (1.22–1.54)	[10]	1.10 (0.99–1.22)	[8]	1.52 (1.34–1.72)	[7]
Asthma prevalence c–c		1.35 (1.19–1.54)	[13]						
Asthma incidence	<6			1.31 (1.22–1.41)	[4]				
Asthma incidence	>6			1.13 (1.04–1.22)	[4]				
Asthma prognosis	<1–8	1.35 (0.87–2.08)	[5]						
Asthma prognosis	<7–16			0.71 (0.57–0.89)	[2]				
Bronchial hyper-reactivity		1.28 (1.08–1.52)	[8]						
Allergic sensitisation		0.88 (0.80–0.98)	[12]						

[n]=number of studies on which pooled odds ratios based

x–s = cross– sectional studies
c–c = case control studies

APPENDIX

Medline Search Strategy

To identify all passive smoking references ($=wildcard):

(a)   MESH heading "Tobacco smoke pollution"

(b)   {passive **OR** second–hand **OR** second hand **OR** involuntary **OR** parent$ **OR** maternal **OR** mother$ **OR** paternal **OR** father$ **OR** household$} **AND** {smok$ **OR** tobacco$ **OR** cigarette$}

(c)   Combine (a) **OR** (b)

To restrict to children:

(1)   Restrict (c) to all relevant age groups

(2)   Search within (c) for:
{Paediatric$ **OR** pedatric$ **OR** infan$ **OR** child$ **OR** adolescen$

(3)   Combine (1) **OR** (2)

EMBASE Search Strategy

Textword searches of titles, keywords and abstracts were carried out as above. That is (b) **AND** (2).

Electronic search strategies for indentifying specific endpoints in Reference Manager

Among references downloaded from Medline or Embase as above, search for any of the following text strings in title, abstract or keyword fields:

Disease	Strings searched for
SIDS	'infant death' **OR** 'SIDS'
Ear	'tympanom' **OR** 'otitis' **OR** 'middle ear' **OR** 'glue ear'
Tonsils	'tonsil'
Allergy'	globulin E' **OR** 'IgE' **OR** 'atopic' **OR** 'atopy' **OR** 'allergy' **OR** 'skin prick'
Spirometry	'lung' **OR** 'fev' **OR** 'pefr' **OR** 'fvc' **OR** 'pulmonary' **OR** 'flow rate' OR 'spirometr'
Asthma	'asthma'
Symptoms	'cough' **OR** 'wheeze' **OR** 'breathless' **OR** 'phlegm' **OR** 'mucous'
Others	'respirat' **OR** 'bronch' **OR** 'pneumon'

ANNEX J

DISEASES WITH LOWER RISKS IN SMOKERS

Sir Richard Doll
Imperial Cancer Research Fund Cancer Studies Unit
Harkness Building, Radcliffe Infirmary, Oxford OX2 6HE

Introduction

When tobacco was first introduced into Europe its use was advocated as a cure and castigated as a cause of many diseases. Little scientific evidence of either was, however, adduced until the 1930s, when serious evidence of the harmful effect of smoking began to accumulate. At first this pointed to the production of cancer, primarily in the lung, but also, to some extent, in the upper respiratory and digestive tracts as a whole. Later, when cohort studies were undertaken, it became clear that smoking was also associated with an increased mortality from many diseases in many different organs. This was at first surprising, but it ceased to be so when it was realized that tobacco smoke contained more than 4000 different chemicals, many of which were readily absorbed from the alveoli and were noxious in animal experiments. That some of them might also be beneficial in counteracting the harmful effects of other agents, or perhaps by making up for physiological deficiencies, should have been equally evident, but it is only in recent years that this possibility has come to be seriously considered. Now, however, there is good evidence that smoking does alleviate or reduce the risk of a few diseases and this needs to be put into balance and weighed against the risk of harm, when attempts are made to assess the total effects of smoking on the public health.

Parkinsonism

Parkinsonism was the first condition that was found to be less common (or less fatal) in smokers than in non-smokers. It was found by Kahn (1966)[1] after following 200,000 US veterans with known smoking habits for 8 years and quickly confirmed in cohort studies of a million American men and women (Hammond, 1966)[2] and 34,000 male British doctors (Doll, personal communication). Kahn's and Hammond's data and later data for 280,000 Japanese followed by Hirayama (1985)[3] and for the British doctors who have now been followed for 40 years (Doll et al., 1994)[4] are summarised in Table 1. All show relative risks for ever smokers less than 1.0 ranging from 0.4 to 0.8.

Further information has been provided in 14 case-control studies, including 12 reviewed by Marmot (1990)[6] and 2 published subsequently (Sasco and Paffenbarger, 1990;[7] Stern et al., 1991[8]). The estimated relative risks ranged from 0.2 to 0.7, 13 were significantly less than 1.0 out of 18 (including some separate estimates for men and women) and the mean was 0.5.

The totality of these observations cannot be due to chance nor to bias nor can the relationship be dismissed as an artefact, as Riggs (1992)[9] has suggested on the grounds that the increased mortality of smokers early in life leaves a higher proportion of non-smokers in old age when Parkinson's disease characteristically occurs. The mathematical models that Riggs employs to bolster his argument are themselves unrealistic and the possibility that he suggests is excluded by the fact that the epidemiological findings are all obtained from studies in which cases and controls have been matched for age.

Table 1: Mortality from Parkinson's Disease by Smoking Habit: Observations in Cohort Studies

Author	Comparison	Relative Risk
Kahn, 1966[1]	Men who had ever smoked cigarettes compared with men who never smoked or smoked very occasionally	0.36[i]
Hammond, 1966[2]	Men with history of "only cigarette smoking" compared with men who had never smoked regularly ages 45-64 years ages 65-79 years	 0.76[ii] 0.81[ii]
Hirayama, 1985[3]	Smokers compared with non smokers	0.6[iii]
Doll et al., 1994[4]	Men who had ever smoked compared with lifelong non-smokers	0.80[iv]

[i]   "40 deaths compared with 112.3 expected".

[ii]   "These rates are unstable statistically due to small numbers observed". (Total Parkinsonism deaths, all habits, 51 underlying cause and 72 contributory cause.)

[iii] Cited by Baron (1986).[5]

[iv]   p<0.01 for trend non-smokers, ex-smokers, current smokers

That smoking should protect against the disease is biologically plausible, as nicotine stimulates the dopamingergic pathways that are characteristically damaged in affected subjects. It should, therefore, be concluded, on the present evidence, that smoking either diminishes the risk of developing the disease or reduces its fatality and that it does so, in either case by between 20 and 50 per cent.

Endometrial Cancer

The idea that the risk of endometrial cancer might be reduced by smoking arose partly because of the knowledge that it reduced the age at menopause and partly because of the findings in case-control studies initially undertaken to test the effect of oestrogens on the risk of the disease. Evidence that smoking does have this effect is compelling. The principal epidemiological evidence from three cohort studies[10,11,12] is summarised in Table 2. The three studies that showed a reduced risk related entirely (Ross et al., 1990)[12] or almost entirely to postmenopausal women, while nearly half the cases in the one study that did not (70 out of 150) related to premenopausal women.

TABLE 2: **Risk of Endometrial Cancer by Smoking Habit: Observations in Cohort Studies**

Risk relative to that in women who never smoked cigarettes			
Author	Current smoker	Ex-smoker	No of cases
Garfinkel, Boffeta (1990)*[10]	0.9	1.1	68
1960-72	0.6	0.7	44
1982-86			
Stampfer et al (1990)†[11]	1.0	1.0	150
Ross et al (1990)†[12]	0.7	0.7	55

* Mortality data. The numbers of cases include only smokers and ex-smokers; number of non smokers not given

† Incidence data

Further evidence has been provided in 16 case-control studies, including nine reviewed by Weiss (1990)[13] and seven published subsequently (Koumantaki et al., 1989;[14] Lawrence et al., 1989;[15] Elliott et al., 1990;[16] Dahlgren et al., 1991;[17] Shu et al., 1991;[18] Brinton et al., 1993;[19] Austin et al., 1993[20]). With one exception the relative risks ranged from 0.5 to 0.8, the exception being a study of 268 affected women in Shanghai in whom the relative risk was 1.7 with 95 per cent confidence limits of 0.9 and 3.0[18]. Other evidence, summarised by Weiss[13] showed that the risk diminished with the amount smoked, and was greater in post-menopausal women than in premenopausal and in oestrogen users than in non-users. Several studies showed that the reduction in risk was not due to confounding with the use of oral contraceptives.

In this case, there is a clear mechanism by which smoking might be expected to have such an effect. The risk of endometrial cancer is directly related to the extent to which the endometrium is exposed to unopposed oestrogen and there is evidence that smoking has a generally anti-oestrogenic effect. It is, for example, associated with increased risks of osteoporosis postmenopausally (Law, 1990)[21] and with decreased risks of fibroids, vomiting in pregnancy, and endometriosis (Ross et al., 1990).[12] Smoking does not materially affect the level of oestrogen in the blood (Barrett-Connor, 1990)[22] but there are other ways in which it might have an anti-oestrogenic effect. One is a modification of the normal metabolism of oestrogen in the blood, in particular by enhancing the hydroxylation of oestrone at the C-2 position rather than the C-16c position, leading to the production of metabolites that are virtually devoid of peripheral oestrogenic activity and are rapidly cleared from the circulation (Michnovitz and Fishman, 1990;[23] Black et al., 1990[24]). Another way is by increasing the secretion of androgens (see Barrett-Connor[22] for review).

On present evidence it should be concluded that smoking reduces the risk of endometrial cancer by about 50 per cent.

Ulcerative Colitis

The idea that smoking might reduce the risk of ulcerative colitis was more surprising. It arose when Harries and his colleagues noticed that very few of their patients with the disease were smokers and sent a questionnaire to 230 patients.[25] Only 8 per cent proved to be current smokers against 44 per cent of the same number of men and women attending a fracture clinic, matched for sex and age. By 1993, the results had been reported of thirteen case-control studies in Britain, Germany, Italy, Sweden, the United States, and Yugoslavia and of two cohort studies in Britain (see Logan, 1990[26] for review and Lorusso et al.,1989;[27] Vucelic et al., 1990;[28] Persson et al., 1990;[29] Samuelsson et al., 1991;[30] Katschinski 1993[31]). All gave odds ratios of less than 1.0 for current smokers, varying from 0.18 to 0.96 in the case-control studies and almost identical ratios of 0.68 and 0.65 in the two cohort studies. The ratios in ex-smokers were, in contrast, consistently greater than 1.0 so that in Logan's review[26] the ratios for men and women who had ever smoked were nearer to 1.0 and led to an estimate of 0.82 with 95% confidence limits of 0.71 and 0.85 for the combined data from eight studies.

Smoking, in contrast is found to be associated with an increased risk of Crohn's disease, which is thought to share a common genetic susceptibility with ulcerative colitis and the interpretation of these findings is obscure. It could be that smoking promotes Crohn's disease in the susceptible population, leaving the non-smokers to develop ulcerative colitis; but why then should the risk in ex-smokers be increased? A direct protective effect seems more likely with the disease relapsing or appearing for the first time when the protective effect is withdrawn. In this case, the benefit is relatively small, the overall reduction in risk from smoking being of the order of 20 per cent.

Other Conditions

No other condition that carries a material risk of death has been shown to be less common in smokers than in non-smokers and, with one possible exception referred to below, it is unlikely that any is likely to be found. In particular, smokers do not have a reduced risk of breast cancer, although one might have been expected because of the anti-oestrogenic effect of smoking (MacMahon, 1990)[32] and Parkinson's disease was the only disease that was negatively related to smoking among the 54 causes or groups of causes of death that were individually responsible for more than 50 deaths in a 40 year follow-up of British doctors with known smoking habits (Doll et al., 1994)[4]. If any other diseases are similarly related, they would not, in that study, have accounted individually for more than 0.25 per cent of the total mortality.

Alzheimer's Disease

The exception that still has to be considered in Alzheimer's disease. A review of eight case-control studies in Australia, Italy, the Netherlands, and the USA (Graves et al., 1991)[33] found a reduced relative risk in seven with an estimated risk from the pooled results of 0.78 that was marginally significant (95% confidence limits 0.62, 0.98), a non significant decreasing risk with amount smoked (p=0.11), and a significantly decreasing risk with the product of duration of smoking and amount smoked (p=0.0003). Information was obtained in all studies from next of kin or other informants in the same way for both cases and controls, but even so there are several opportunities for bias in such studies that make it difficult to accept the results at face value. The difference between cases and controls was more marked in the older group (70 years of age and older) in which alone it was statistically significant and it is possible that older patients with Alzheimer's disease who smoked were differentially screened out, as a result of the presence of morbid conditions associated with smoking (through for example, early death or differential hospitalisation). A similar result was obtained in a study of 31 pairs of monozygous and 10 pairs of dizygous twins, discordant for Alzheimer's disease (Bharucha et al., 1986)[34] and when data from both sets were combined, the relative risk in cigarette smokers was 0.4 (p, one sided, <0.05). Here again, however, there is the possibility that the result was an artefact, as information about deceased twins was obtained from relatives and the comparison was apparently not limited, as it should have been, to unaffected twins that were know to have been alive at the time the affected twin's disease was diagnosed.

Neuropharmacological mechanisms exist by which smoking might be thought to delay the onset of the disease, as in the case of Parkinsonism, but it cannot be concluded that smoking reduces the risk until a reduction is also seen in cohort studies, based on smoking histories given by the subjects themselves before the disease appeared. One such study has been reported from the USA. Herbert et al., (1992)[35] took advantage of the data collected for one of the four Established Populations for Epidemiologic Study of the Elderly that had been sponsored by the National Institute on Aging. Participants had been interviewed twice, with an interval of three years between interviews, which enabled them to be classified by degree of memory loss. Herbert and his colleagues were, therefore, able to select a stratified random sample of 690 individuals, weighted to provide a high proportion with some degree of memory loss. Thirty two died before the study could be completed and 513 (78 per cent of the remainder) had a thorough neuropsychiatric examination. Probable Alzheimer's disease was diagnosed in 76. After allowance for sex, age, use of alcohol, and education, the odds ratio for ever smoked cigarettes was 0.7 with 95 per cent confidence limits of 0.3 and 1.4.

Much more information is likely to be obtained about Alzheimer's disease in the next few years. It will not be easy to interpret, partly for the reasons given above (it is derived from case-control studies) and partly because the death rate at old ages is so high that the difference between the rates in cigarette smokers and non-smokers may require age-standardisation to be carried out by single years of age. If it proves, as it may do, that cigarette smoking helps to delay the onset of Alzheimer's disease, this may be of some practical assistance to research into the mechanism by which the disease is produced and into methods by which the disease can be treated. If, however, other forms of dementia (due, for example, to microvascular disease) are made more common by smoking (as they may be too), there may be no overall benefit in relation to dementia to put into scales against the harmful effects of smoking. That such may be the case is suggested by the results of a 40 year follow-up of British doctors with known smoking habits (Doll et al.,).[4] Too few deaths (19) were certified as due to Alzheimer's disease to provide useful information specifically for that disease, but it is notable that the annual age standardized mortality attributed to dementia, based on 100 deaths, about half of which are likely to have been due to Alzheimer's disease, was slightly higher in those who had ever smoked (11 per 100,000 per year) than in those who had never smoked (9 per 100,000 per year).

Premature Deaths Avoided By Smoking

No precise estimate can be made of the number of premature deaths that have been avoided in this country as a result of smoking, but an approximate estimate can be made from the figures cited above for the effect of smoking on the risks of Parkinson's disease (reduced by 20-50 per cent), endometrial cancer (reduced by 50 per cent), and ulcerative colitis (reduced by 20 per cent). In Britain, in 1990 these diseases accounted, respectively, for 4401, 1587 and 199 deaths (including all deaths attributed to cancer of the uterus unspecified with cancer of the corpous uteri). If we assume that 50 per cent of the population had been smokers, the number of premature deaths avoided by smoking could have been between 1000 and 2000. This compares with 138,000 deaths which, according to Peto et al., (1994),[36] were attributable to smoking in the UK in the same year.

Acknowlegement

The author is grateful to Professor Richard Peto for his help in preparing this paper.

References

1.   Kahn H A. The Dorn study of smoking and mortality among US veterans: report on eight and one half years of observation. In: Haenszel W, ed. *Epidemiological approaches to the study of cancer and other chronic diseases.* Maryland: National Cancer Institute, 1996; 1-125. (National Cancer Institute, monograph 19).

2.   Hammond E C. Smoking in relation to the death rates of one million men and women. In: W. Haenszel, ed. *Epidemiological approaches to the study of cancer and other chronic diseases.* Maryland: National Cancer Institute, 1966; 127-204. (National Cancer Institute, monograph 19).

3.   Hirayama T. Epidemiologic patterns of Parkinson's disease based on a cohort study. In: *Epidemiology of Intractable Diseases Research Committee.* Tokyo: Japan Ministry of Health & Welfare, 1985.

4.   Doll R, Peto R, Wheatley et al. Mortality in relation to smoking: 40 years' observations on male British doctors. *BMJ* 1994; **309**: 901-11.

5.   Baron J A. Cigarette smoking and Parkinson's disease. *Neurology* 1986; **36**: 1490-6.

6.   Marmot M. Smoking and Parkinson's disease.   In: N. Wald, J. Baron, eds. *Smoking and hormone related disorders.*   Oxford: Oxford University Press, 1990; 135-41.

7.   Sasco A J, Paffenbarger R S. Jr.   Smoking and Parkinson's disease. *Epidemiology* 1990; **1**: 460-65.

8.   Stern M, Dulaney E, Gruber S B et al.   The epidemiology of Parkinson's disease. *Ann Neurol* 1991; **48**: 903-7.

9.   Riggs J E. Cigarette smoking and Parkinson disease: the illusion of a neuroprotective effect. *Clin Neuropharmacol* 1992; **15**: 88-99.

10.   Garfinkel L, Boffeta P. Smoking and oestrogen-related sites: data from American Cancer Society studies. In: N. Wald, J Baron, eds. *Smoking and hormone-related disorders.* Oxford: Oxford University Press, 1990; 1-19.

11.   Stampfer M J, Colditz G A, London S J et al.   Smoking and hormone related disorders in the Nurses Health Study. In: N. Wald, J. Baron, eds. *Smoking and hormone related disorders.* Oxford: Oxford University Press, 1990; 20-31.

12.   Ross R K, Bernstein L, Pagannini-Hilla et al.   Effects of cigarette smoking on hormone-related diseases in a Southern California retirement community.   In: N. wald, J. Baron, eds. *Smoking and hormone related disorders.*   Oxford: Oxford University Press, 1990; 32-56.

13.   Weiss N S.   Cigarette smoking and the incidence of endometrial cancer.   In: N. Wald, J. Baron, editors.   *Smoking and hormone related disorders.*   Oxford: Oxford University Press 1990; 145-54.

14.   Koumantaki Y, Tzonou A, Koumantakis E et al.   A case-control study of cancer of the endometrium in Athens.   *Int J Cancer* 1989; **43:** 795-9.

15.   Lawrence C, Tessaro I, Durgerian S et al. Advanced stage endometrial cancer: contributions of estrogen use, smoking, and other risk factors.   *Gynecol Oncol* 1989; **32**: 41-5.

16.   Elliott E A, Matanoski G M, Rosenshein N B et al.   Body fat patterning in women with endometrial cancer. *Gynecol Oncol* 1990; **39**: 253-8.

17.   Dahlgren E, Friberg L G, Johansson et al. Endometrial carcinoma; ovarian dysfunction: a risk factor in young women.   *Eur J Obstet Gynecol Reprod Biol* 1991; **41**: 143-50.

18.   Shu X O, Brinton L A, Zheng W et al.   A population based case-control study of endometrial cancer in Shanghai. *Int J Cancer* 1991; **49**: 38-43.

19.   Brinton L A, Barrett R J, Berman M L et al.   Cigarette smoking and the risk of endometrial cancer. *Am J Epidemiol* 1993; **137**: 281 -91.

20.   Austin H, Drews C, Partridge E E.   A case-control study of endometrial cancer in relation to cigarette smoking, serum estrogen levels, and alcohol use.   *Am J Obstet Gynecol* 1993; **169**: 1086-10.

21.   Law M.   Smoking and osteoporosis.   In: N. Wald, J Baron, eds.   *Smoking and hormone-related disorders.*   Oxford: Oxford University Press 1990; 83-92.

22.   Barrett-Connor E.   Smoking and endogenous sex hormones in men and women. In: N. Wald, J. Baron, eds. *Smoking and hormone-related diseases.* Oxford: Oxford University Press 1990; 183-96.

23.   Michnovitz J J, Fishman J.   Increased oxidative metabolism of oestrogens in male and female smokers. In: N. Wald, J. Baron, eds.   *Smoking and hormone-related disorders.* Oxford: Oxford University Press 1990; 197-207.

24.   Black D, Balls, Forrester L, et al. Oestrogen 2-hydroxylation in rat and human liver. In: N. Wald, J. Baron, eds. *Smoking and hormone-related disorders.* Oxford: Oxford University Press 1990; 253-6.

25.   Harries A D, Baird A, Rhodes J.   Non-smoking: a feature of ulcerative colitis. *BMJ* 1982; **284**: 706.

26.   Logan R F A.   Smoking and inflammatory bowel disease.   In: N. Wald, J. Baron, eds. *Smoking and hormone related disorders.*   Oxford: Oxford University Press 1990; 122-34.

27.   Lorusso D, Leo S, Misciagna G et al.   Cigarette smoking and ulcerative colitis: a case-control study. *Hepato-gastroenterology* 1989; **36**: 202-4.

28.   Vucelic B. Korac B. Sentic M et al.   Cigarette smoking and ulcerative colitis-is there a causal relationship? *Lijec-Vjesn* 1990; **112**: 203-26.

29.   Persson P G, Ahlbom A, Hellers G.   Inflammatory bowel disease and tobacco smoke - a case-control study. *Gut* 1990; **31**: 1377-81.

30.   Samuelsson S M, Ekbom A, Zack C G et al. Risk factors for extensive ulcerative colitis and ulcerative proctitis: a population based case-control study. *Gut* 1991; **32**: 1526-30.

31.   Katschinski B. Smoking and ovulation inhibitor in inflammatory bowel diseases. *Med Klin* 1993; **85** (Suppl. 1): 5-8.

32.   MacMahon B.   Cigarette smoking and cancer of the breast. In: N. Wald, J. Baron, eds. *Smoking and hormone related disorders.*   Oxford: Oxford University Press 1990; 154-66.

33.   Graves A B, Van Duijn C M, Chandra V et al. Alcohol and tobacco consumption as risk factors for Alzheimer's disease: a collaborative reanalysis of case-control studies. *Int J Epidemiol* 1991; **20** (Suppl.2): S48-557.

34.   Bharucha N E, Stokes L, Schoenberg B S et al. A case-control study of twin pairs discordant for Parkinson's disease: a search for environment risk factors. *Neurology*, 1986; **36**: 284-7.

35.   Herbert L E, Scherp P A, Beckett L A et al. Relation of smoking and alcohol consumption to incident Alzheimer's disease. *Am J Epidemiol.* 1992; **135**: 347-55.

36.   Peto R, Lopez A D, Boreham J et al. *Mortality from smoking in developed countries.* Oxford: Oxford University Press, 1994.

ANNEX K

VOLUNTARY AGREEMENT ON THE APPROVAL AND USE OF NEW ADDITIVES IN TOBACCO PRODUCTS IN THE UK

Made 7th March 1997

Furnished to the Office of Fair Trading pursuant to section 24 of the Restrictive Trade Practices Act 1976

Signed . . . .

On behalf of the Secretary of State for Health

VOLUNTARY AGREEMENT ON THE APPROVAL AND USE OF NEW ADDITIVES IN TOBACCO PRODUCTS IN THE UK

The Tobacco Manufacturers represented by the Tobacco Manufacturers' Association and the members of the Imported Tobacco Products Advisory Council have agreed with the Department of Health to follow the arrangements set out in the following Agreement. This agreement replaces the provisions relating to additives in the 1984 Voluntary Agreement on Tobacco Product Modification and Research.

The provisions of the agreement cover additives to cigarettes, hand-rolling tobacco, cigars and pipe tobacco as defined in Section 2 of the Voluntary Agreement.

This agreement will stand until at least 10 years from date of agreement with provision for amendment in the light of any United Kingdom legislation necessary to enact European Community legislation.

If any provision of this agreement would cause this agreement to be subject to registration under the Restrictive Trade Practices Act 1976, then that provision will not take effect until the day after particulars of the agreement have been furnished to the Director General of Fair Trading pursuant to Section 24 of that Act.

This agreement has been notified to the European Commission in line with Directive 83/189/EEC.

Dated the 7th day of March 1997

Signed for, and on behalf of, the Tobacco Manufacturers' Association

....

Signed for, and on behalf of, the Imported Tobacco Products Advisory Council

....

Signed for, and on behalf of, the Secretary of State for Health

....

Signed for, and on behalf of, the Secretary of State for Scotland

....

Signed for, and on behalf of, the Secretary of State for Northern Ireland

....

Signed for, and on behalf of, the Secretary of State for Wales

VOLUNTARY AGREEMENT ON THE APPROVAL AND USE OF NEW ADDITIVES IN TOBACCO PRODUCTS IN THE UK

1. Introduction

1.1 The scrutiny of additives rests with the Department of Health, acting on behalf of the UK Health Departments, taking advice from the Scientific Committee on Tobacco and Health (SCOTH) and its Technical Advisory Group (TAG) (or any successor committees) as appropriate.

1.2 The companies and the Department agree to comply with the arrangements set out in this agreement and with the procedure for obtaining approval for new additives set out in the guidelines at Appendix 1.

1.3 All information supplied to the Department will be treated in the strictest confidence.

2. Definition

2.1 An additive is any substance added by the tobacco manufacturer in the course of manufacture of a smoking product and intended to be burnt. The term "additive" relates to any substance other than water but excluding reconstituted sheet made wholly from tobacco. It includes all additives added to cigarette papers by the tobacco manufacturer, adhesives to cigarette paper and cigar seams and also includes tobacco processing agents used in the course of tobacco manufacture.

2.2 The guidelines at Appendix 1 apply to all new additives defined in Section 2.1 of this agreement. It is recognised that, in the case of new processing agents leaving no free or measurable residue and with no intentional use in the finished product, the submission may only need to demonstrate this fact.

2.3 Imprinting inks and additives to tips, filters, filter wrappers and overwrappers may continue to be used without reference to the Department.

2.4 Existing substances currently used in adhesives to cigarette paper and cigar seams, and processing agents, may continue to be used but manufacturers will supply the Department with a list of adhesives and processing agents currently in use in order that the Department may compile a historical list as for other additives.

3. Arrangements

3.1 United Kingdom manufacturers and importers should not use non-approved additives in products marketed for sale to the public in the United Kingdom. All UK duty-free sales are excluded from the scope of this agreement.

3.2   Companies manufacturing, or importing, tobacco products marketed for consumption in the UK have the responsibility to ensure that any additive used in any of these products:

(a)   has been approved through the Department of Health or appears in the published list of permitted additives or is authorised by another EU Member State (see Section 3.9); and

(b)   conforms with the usage limits specified by the Department of Health and that collectively the additives are within the aggregate usage limits and are only used for the approved product style.

Companies wishing to use an additive which is authorised by another EU Member State but not previously approved through the Department of Health will notify the Department accordingly with the relevant information (see Appendix 3).

3.3   Any additives on the permitted list may be used, up to the approved level, without reference to the Department.

3.4   As a matter of routine, the Department needs UK manufacturers and importers to confirm annually that the additive usage in each tobacco product is within the individual and aggregate limits set out in the list of permitted additives or as approved by the Department. The form of this confirmation is at Appendix 2.

3.5   There may also be occasions when the Department needs information on the extent and level of use of a particular additive or combination of additives to tobacco products marketed for consumption in the UK. UK manufacturers and importers will ensure that such requests are dealt with promptly (whether they relate to new additives or additives on the permitted list). Such information will only be sought by the Department in relation to specific public health concerns and will remain strictly in confidence within the Department.

3.6   UK manufacturers and importers are not required to inform the Department of any changes in the amount of use within the agreed usage limits.

3.7   This agreement does not affect any responsibility of the UK manufacturer or importer for its products.

3.8   Companies will notify the Department when newly approved additives are included in products at the time when the products are first offered for sale to the public in the United Kingdom. Such information will remain strictly in confidence within the Department.

3.9   Those additives which are authorised by another EU Member State following assessment by a recognised scientific body, for use in the manufacture of tobacco products covered by this agreement, shall also be considered to conform with these guidelines as long as the authorisation to use the additive has been published in an official publication accessible to members of the public with an interest. The information required by the Department of Health in relation to such additives is set out in Appendix 3.

4.   Publication of Information

4.1   The Department will maintain a list of approved additives with details of individual and aggregate usage limits. The list will be added to and amended in the light of submissions and notifications made by companies and other evidence available. The existence of the list will be publicised by means of a notice in the London Gazette and copies will be available from the Department. An additive will only be reported in the published list six months after it has been included in a product offered for sale in the United Kingdom unless the company has requested, in writing, that the six months' period be waived and the additive be included in the public list immediately.

APPENDIX 1

GUIDELINES FOR TESTING AND USE OF NEW ADDITIVES IN TOBACCO PRODUCTS IN THE UK

Introduction

1. The following guidelines set out the arrangements for the approval of new additives to tobacco products.

2. For additives not already approved, or approved for a particular product style, or if some increase in usage limit is sought, companies will make a submission to the Department in accordance with these guidelines.

3. Individuals should not be needlessly exposed to new substances or novel uses of other substances. UK manufacturers and importers should provide the Department with sufficient information to enable it to agree inclusion and determine limits of inclusion in the finished product.

4. Submissions, and requests for information, will be based on sound toxicological information and scientifically based judgement. When the Department is not content with the scope of information provided, it will request specific additional information or clarification.

5. Following assessment, the Department may:

    (a) give permission to use and set a usage limit. The limit will be based on toxicological evidence although it may be set lower than the highest toxicologically acceptable level. UK manufacturers and importers may not exceed this level without making a further submission. The Department may also set aggregate limits for the total level of additives in the final product;

    (b) not give permission to use. This may be because:

        (i) the results of toxicity testing are unsatisfactory; or

        (ii) acceptability cannot be judged on the basis of the information provided. The Department may seek additional information from the manufacturer; in that case, either a provisional recommendation will be made or the recommendation will be delayed until additional information is available.

Timing of Submissions

6. UK manufacturers and importers should not seek permission to use an additive not on the permitted list until they have a serious intention of using it in a tobacco product. Where there are no complicating factors the Department will be able to reply promptly to the submission.

7. The Department recognises that consumer acceptability tests can avoid unnecessary work in the production and consideration of full submissions on additives that are subsequently found to be unacceptable in such tests. Companies may carry out limited consumer testing, involving the provision of no more than 100 cigarettes to any individual smoker, without approaching the Department.

8. Permission for more extensive consumer testing prior to seeking formal approval for an additive will be given by the Department providing that an assessment by a suitably qualified toxicologist is supplied, indicating that there is no apparent acute hazard to those participating. Participants must be volunteers, aware that they may in the course of the test be exposed to a non-approved substance, and must be tested according to guidelines set out in the Report of the Royal College of Physicians on Research on Healthy Volunteers.[1] The Department will normally reply within 30 days of the receipt of requests to carry out consumer testing. The Department may set limits on the level of individual exposure in such tests. If such limits are set, the manufacturer should not undertake any more extensive consumer testing until the Department has considered a full submission.

Form of Submission

9. The information which may be needed for the assessment and acceptance of new additives to tobacco is listed below. Some of the information requirements may not be relevant to particular substances. It will help in the consideration of submissions if companies explain why they have omitted particular information. Submissions should provide sufficient information to demonstrate to the Department's satisfaction that the additive would not increase the hazard of the product. Additives may be used for any reasonable purpose provided they are shown to be safe. The Secretariat will be happy to discuss requirements in advance of receiving a submission.

a. **Composition of the Additive to be Used**
    Examination of the structure of a substance may aid in assessing its potential toxicity. It is essential that the structure, or specification, or both, of the substance is clearly defined and is analytically and toxicologically comparable to that which will be used in the final product.

b. **Purpose of Using the Additive**
    When seeking to use an additive it is desirable that the purpose of use should be detailed.

c. **Status in Food, Tobacco and Drug Laws**
    There is a wealth of toxicological data with respect to additives used in food, drugs, cosmetics and other consumer products. However, when considering the use of such additives in tobacco products, it is necessary to demonstrate that such data is relevant to its use in material intended to be burnt and inhaled.

d. **The Quantity to be Used**
    The level of toxicity assessment is dependent on the quantity which may be received. Relevant toxicological data should be submitted which will allow the Department to set a maximum safe level of use or determine if a level requested is acceptable.

---

[1] Research on Healthy Volunteers: A Report of the Royal College of Physicians. Journal of the Royal College of Physicians of London Vol. 20 No.4 October 1986.

e. **Details of its Quantitative Transference to Smoke**
Chemical analytical details will be required of the transference to smoke of the original substance.

f. **Destructive Distillation, Pyrolysis and Formulation of Potentially Noxious Components**
It is important that as much information as is reasonable and technically possible should be given. An explanation should be provided if no data is supplied eg if the residue is too small to be measurable.

g. **Biological Studies**
These studies would be performed after the amount to be used, its transference to smoke, and its principal metabolites are known. The Secretariat will provide advice when such studies are being planned by manufacturers and importers. However, in principle, the following would be necessary:

An Inhalational Study (Pyrolysed Tobacco Product)
Classically this should be of 90 days duration but a shorter/longer duration may be appropriate depending on the factors mentioned above.

Full details must be supplied eg:

> Body Weight Data
> Clinical Observations
> Haematology
> Clinical Chemistry
> Macroscopical Data
> Organ Weight Data
> Histopathology of Major Organs

It is recommended that a draft protocol is submitted to the Secretariat before the work commences.

Genotoxicity
This should be carried out on:

a. The substance itself (including, where relevant, in pyrolysed form);

b. The condensate of a reference cigarette containing the substance

The tests required should be conducted in accordance with the Committee of Mutagenicity's Guidelines (Chapter 7).

METHODOLOGY

10. The Department will keep the guidelines under review and wherever possible, particularly in relation to paragraph 9(g), recommend methodology that obviates the need for animal testing.

APPENDIX 2

CERTIFICATE OF COMPLIANCE_____

1. The Department of Health, under Section 3.4 of this Agreement, will hold a register of UK tobacco manufacturers and importers of cigarettes, cigars, hand-rolling tobacco and pipe tobaccos marketed for consumption in the UK. The UK tobacco manufacturers and importers will notify the Department of Health of the names of persons who will provide certificates of conformance for such products and will notify the Department of any subsequent changes of names of such persons.

2. Annual Certificates of Compliance (in the form atttached) will be completed by the relevant tobacco companies party to this voluntary agreement and signed by a company representative with appropriate authority.

VOLUNTARY AGREEMENT ON ADDITIVES

ANNUAL CERTIFICATE OF COMPLIANCE FOR

[insert name of manufacturer]

It is hereby confirmed that all tobacco products, being for these purposes any cigarettes, hand-rolling tobacco, cigars and pipe tobacco, produced by the Company ("the Company") between [date of signature] 1997 and [following year] 1998 complied with the provisions of the Voluntary Agreement on the Approval and Use of New Additives in Tobacco Products in the UK as agreed on *[x   1997 - date of signature]* ("the Agreement").

It is further confirmed that during the above certified period, all additives added by the Company in the course of tobacco manufacture, (as defined by Section 2.1 of the Agreement) were:-

(a)   on the Department of Health's published permitted list or as approved by the Department;

(b)   within the maximum usage limits as specified by the Department of Heath;

(c)   collectively within the aggregate usage limits as specified by the Department of Health; and

(d)   used only for the product style in respect of which they have been approved.

It is hereby confirmed that the Company will continue to abide by the provisions of the Agreement.

Signed: **Dated:**

Position in Company:

APPENDIX 3

NOTIFICATION OF EU AUTHORISED ADDITIVES _____

1. The Department of Health, as required under European Directive 83/189/EEC, and as set out in Section 3.9, will raise no objection to the use in products for consumption in the United Kingdom of an additive authorised by another EU member state. This is subject to the receipt of the following information from the manufacturer or importer who wishes to use such an additive:

    i. The status of the tobacco additive in the specified EU Member State's tobacco legislation, including any maximum inclusion levels.

    ii. Any summary information concerning the current national and international status of the additives in non-tobacco consumer products.

    iii. Details of the proposed use of the tobacco additive by product type:

        ■ cigarette/RYO

        ■ cigar;

        ■ pipe tobacco.

    iv. Details of the proposed purpose of the tobacco additive under the following headings:

        ■ casing or flavouring ingredient;

        ■ solvent, for the application of additive;

        ■ tobacco sheet additive;

        ■ cigarette paper additive;

        ■ cigarette paper seam adhesive;

        ■ cigar wrapper or binder seam adhesive;

        ■ tobacco processing agent; or

        ■ other, eg, preservative.

    v. Specify, if other than solvent or tobacco processing agent, whether the additive should be classified "List 1" (individually present at levels at or above 0.1%) or "List 2" (individually present at levels below 0.1%) as defined in the Department's Permitted List of Additives to Tobacco Products.

2.   Where an additive has been approved for use in the UK on the basis of EU mutual recognition, this will be indicated in the Department of Health's published list of approved additives.

3.   Manufacturers and importers may use *extractables of tobacco*, without prior approval by the Department of Health, where these have been applied to tobacco for aroma and flavour purposes and as long as the nicotine content of the finished tobacco is not measurably increased by the application of such extractables.

ANNEX L

SCIENTIFIC COMMITTEE ON TOBACCO AND HEALTH TECHNICAL ADVISORY GROUP

Review of Emissions in Cigarette Smoke

Introduction

1. For more than 20 years successive Governments have taken various courses of action to encourage smokers to stop smoking and non-smokers not to start. At the same time a programme of product modification has allowed smokers, unable to give up, to smoke products with reduced emissions. This paper summarises a review undertaken by the Technical Advisory Group (TAG) of the Scientific Committee on Tobacco and Health (SCOTH) to examine the impact on health of this programme, updating earlier work.[1,2,3]

Tar

2. The product modification programme, and subsequent EU regulations, have had a significant impact on tar yields over the past few decades. Typical UK cigarettes had tar yields of about 25-35 mg per cigarette during the 1950s and about 5-15 mg per cigarette in 1990.[4] The sales weighted average tar yield of cigarettes has shown a continuous steady decline through the last three decades, from 20.8 mg in 1972 to 11 mg in 1993.[5] UK Regulations, based on an EC Directive, placed an upper limit of 15 mg of tar per cigarette from the end of 1992, falling to 12 mg from the end of 1997.

3. Although lower tar cigarettes still cause health problems, there is reasonably good evidence to show that, with respect to lung cancer, lower tar cigarettes are less carcinogenic than higher tar cigarettes. For example, the decrease in male lung cancer mortality in England and Wales since the 1960s is consistent with an effect of reduced tar yield, beyond a simple reduction in male smoking prevalence. In 1988 the Independent Scientific Committee on Smoking and Health (ISCSH) concluded that "Smoking lower tar cigarettes confers a reduced risk of lung cancer than does the smoking of cigarettes with the relatively high yields that were customary twenty five or more years ago".[1]

4. Two studies which examined the impact on health of reduced tar have provided further evidence. Tang et al, combining mortality data from a number of prospective studies in the UK in relation to the tar yield of cigarettes, showed that about one quarter of deaths from coronary heart disease, lung cancer, and possibly other smoking related diseases, could be avoided by switching from historically high 30 mg tar cigarettes to those yielding 15 mg tar.[6] Parish et al assessed the impact of smoking cigarettes of different tar yields on the incidence of non-fatal myocardial infarction (MI) and showed that the overall relative risk of suffering a non-fatal MI is 10% higher for smokers of medium tar cigarettes (mean tar yield 13.3 mg per cigarette) compared with smokers of low tar cigarettes (mean tar yield 7.5 mg per cigarette).[7]

5. Both studies investigated smokers who were likely to have smoked products with higher tar yields earlier in their lives. The impact of tar reduction could, therefore, be greater when comparing risks in lifetime smokers of higher and lower tar cigarettes. However, it cannot be stated strongly enough that tar reduction is no substitute for not smoking, as the adverse impact of smoking on disease regardless of cigarette type is clearly demonstrated in each of these studies.

6. When considering the effectiveness of the tar reduction programme, information on dosimetry should be taken into account. Exposure to tobacco smoke may be estimated by measuring levels of cotinine, a nicotine metabolite, in blood, saliva or urine. Some compensatory smoking of lower-yielding products does occur, but unless smokers deliberately remove filters or block ventilation holes, there is increasing difficulty in compensating up to former doses of nicotine and consequently of tar.[8]

7. The prevalence of smoking is strongly linked with socio-economic status, being highest in more deprived groups.[9] There are indications that such factors also influence brand choice and smoke uptake. Socio-economic factors exert independent effects on morbidity and mortality and this could affect the interpretation of data on relationships between yields of tar and relative risks for smoking related diseases.

8. Over the last few years there has been a steady increase in the proportion of smokers reporting they smoke low tar brands of manufactured cigarettes. In 1986 some 19% smoked low tar brands (under 10 mg per cigarette) increasing to 25% in 1992 and 32% in 1994.[9] This trend is due partly to deliberate switching by smokers and partly to the decline in tar yields of all manufactured brands.

9. The increase in popularity of low tar brands is partly offset by an increased prevalence in the smoking of hand-rolled cigarettes. Between 1986 and 1992 prevalence was steady, with 18% of male and 2% of female smokers smoking mainly hand-rolled cigarettes. In 1994 this increased to 21% and 4%, respectively.[9] Recent studies show that a significant proportion of tar yields from hand-rolled cigarettes can be greater than the current maximum limit of 15 mg per cigarette for commercial cigarettes,[10,11] although due to the variable nature of the product, measurement of tar yields from hand-rolled cigarettes is not straightforward. A study undertaken by the Laboratory of the Government Chemist[10] showed that few UK hand-rolled cigarette smokers use filters and high-porosity papers, both of which have played an important part in reducing tar yields in commercial products.

Nicotine

10. Nicotine is addictive and it is this fact which is largely responsible for the continuation of smoking and the consequent exposure to the harmful effects of tar. The perpetuation of the smoking habit results in a wide range of health effects. No previous or current UK regulations have addressed nicotine yields directly. Under current Labelling Regulations, the yield of nicotine, as well as tar, is specified on packets, but no upper limit is set for nicotine. In mainstream smoke nicotine is present in the particulate phase and most cigarette design measures, used to control tar, should also control nicotine. However, for much of the 1970s and 1980s, whilst average tar yields were falling, average nicotine yields did not fall in proportion.[1] This appears to have been brought about through blending tobaccos, increasing the proportion of material with a high nicotine content.

18. It is important to consider the possible impact of reductions in nicotine yield and changes in the ratio of tar:nicotine yields on existing smokers. Large numbers of smokers are addicted to nicotine and altering nicotine levels in middle range cigarettes will not change this. Lowering nicotine yields may increase the health risks of existing smokers who compensate by smoking more, thereby increasing their intake of tar. On balance, however, there is no clear indication regarding advantages or disadvantages of varying the tar:nicotine ratio and the preferred option may be to ensure that tar and nicotine yields fall in line with one another.

19. Issues for consideration if control of nicotine yields is contemplated are:

i) the role of nicotine in smoking-related diseases,

ii) the role of nicotine in addiction and establishing an addictive threshold,

iii) factors influencing smoke uptake, such as pH, smoking patterns and nicotine absorption.

The Health Survey for England could provide a valuable means of monitoring what actually happens in terms of nicotine uptake in the population at large. In some of these annual surveys cotinine determinations have been made on the blood samples taken from participants. So far, data are available from the surveys in 1993 and 1994,[16] and show no appreciable change in cotinine levels among smokers over a one year interval. Continuation of the series could demonstrate to what extent compensatory smoking off-sets the potential benefits of the further reductions anticipated to meet the new tar limits from 1998. Further insight into yield/uptake relationships would be obtained if brands smoked were also recorded for all subjects providing blood samples.

Carbon Monoxide

20. Carbon monoxide is a poisonous gas and contributes nothing to the flavour or "satisfaction" of smoking. It is however an inevitable component of the slow combustion process of tobacco smoking. Although CO has not been regulated, yields of CO have declined, but at a slower rate than tar yields. Some methods of tar reduction, notably filtration, have little or no effect on yields of CO and other gases. Other methods that dilute smoke, such as increased paper porosity and use of ventilation holes, reduce gases as well as particulates. However, yields of CO have fallen less than those of tar over the past few decades, tending to increase the CO:tar ratio.[15]

21. Smoking is the commonest reason for raised carboxyhaemoglobin (COHb) levels in the blood and direct or indirect measurements of COHb are widely used as a test for recent (same day) smoking.[17] Levels in smokers are typically around 6-7% but can rise to 11% or more. Acute cerebral effects occur at much higher levels, (e.g. malfunctioning heating appliances or exposure to car exhaust in confined spaces) and are usually the result of accidents. Levels due to smoking have been shown to be within the range seen in experimental studies to reduce the time to angina pain in exercising patients suffering from heart disease.[18] Endogenously produced carbon monoxide within the central nervous system and in the circulation may serve as a regulator of normal function. Adverse effects of carbon monoxide may, therefore, be linked to the high levels of exposure seen with accidental poisoning but there remains uncertainty of its role at low levels of chronic exposure.

22. Any further action to reduce tar is likely to involve measures such as increased ventilation or changes in the porosity of the cigarette paper, both of which will have a diluting effect on CO. Consequently, separate action to reduce CO yields is probably unnecessary.

Oxides of nitrogen.

23. In addition to carbon monoxide, nitric oxide (NO) is a notable constituent of the gas phase of tobacco smoke. Nitric oxide is produced by the decomposition of nitrates in tobacco, rather than by the combination of atmospheric nitrogen and oxygen, as occurs in sources such as gas flames or internal combustion engines. In cigarettes the oxide produced initially, and inhaled by the smoker, is NO, whereas other sources of oxides of nitrogen usually produce some nitrogen dioxide (NO_2). Although NO exhaled by the smoker or contained in sidestream smoke, once dispersed in a room, will gradually oxidise to NO_2, the smoker receives only NO. The physiological effects of NO and NO_2 are quite different. Inhaled NO appears to have no direct toxic effect whilst NO_2 is a respiratory irritant. However, recent research suggests that smoking adversely affects the physiological function of endogenous NO.[19]

24. NO in cigarettes is related to tobacco type rather than cigarette design. For a given tobacco blend, NO is reduced, along with CO and other gases, by increasing ventilation or paper porosity. Blends containing air-cured tobacco, which is relatively rich in nitrates, produce higher yields of NO than flue-cured tobaccos.[1]

25. The relationship between yields of carbon- and nitrogen-derived noxa and tar is interesting. Work conducted for the former ISCSH showed that yields of carbon-derived noxa followed those of tar, reasonably closely, correlation coefficients being between 0.6 and 0.9 in the survey of 75 brands.[1,20] This relationship should now be re-examined as tar yields have reduced by around 20% since the work was undertaken. Yields of nitrogen-derived noxa are independent of tar yields and relate to type of tobacco and its nitrate content.

26. Apart from nicotine, carbon monoxide and oxides of nitrogen, there are over 4,000 compounds present in the gaseous and particulate phases of tobacco. The specific role of other noxa in smoking-related diseases is poorly understood and research to link yields of other noxa to smoking-related diseases is limited. In addition, experimental toxicity data on other compounds present in tobacco smoke is often based on routes of administration other than inhalation, making extrapolation of results difficult.

27. In the 1960s the American tobacco industry embarked on a programme to reduce the carcinogenic effects of cigarette smoke by reducing levels of carbon-derived polynuclear aromatic hydrocarbons (PAHs) and related compounds in tar. This was achieved not only through cigarette design parameters, but also by using blends of tobacco rich in nitrate which inhibit the formation of these compounds during pyrolysis. Experimental evidence shows that the tar from nitrate-rich tobacco and containing reduced yields of PAHs and phenolic compounds is less carcinogenic than that from tobaccos rich in carbon and low in nitrate.[21] While data from US epidemiological studies show smaller increments in lung cancer mortality in relation to dose, e.g. the number of cigarettes smoked per day,[22] it is not clear whether this is linked to differences in the characteristics of the tobacco or to differences in smoking behaviour like discarding longer butts.

28.   Air-cured tobacco blends are less popular with UK smokers, but consideration should be given to whether there could be any potential benefits in moving towards such blends. Nitrate-rich tobaccos yield higher levels of N-nitroso compounds than other tobaccos. Although tobacco specific nitrosamines are potent carcinogens in animals, their role in the development of smoking-associated cancers in humans is unknown.

29.   A large amount of data on the effects of tobacco cultivation, cigarette design and man-ufacture was taken into account during the course of this review and additional research has been carried out since publication of these data. Modern processing technologies, such as homogenised leaf curing, expanded tobacco and reconstituted tobacco sheet production, may provide scope for both quantitative and qualitative reductions in tobac-co smoke emissions. The introduction of synthetic tobacco substitutes into cigarettes, which was the subject of extensive toxicological work in the late 1960s and early 1970s,[1] proved to be a commercial failure, despite promising results in terms of reduced car-cinogenicity in animal experiments, but other radical changes in cigarette design might be contemplated by industry.

Conclusions

30.   Having considered the data available on emissions in cigarette smoke, the Technical Advisory Group came to the following conclusions.

i)   **Tar**:- The tar content of cigarette smoke is the single most important factor in terms of health risk. Tar reduction reduces the risk of developing some smok-ing-related diseases, notably lung cancer. However, this is small and does not compare with the benefit derived from giving up smoking altogether. Consumer acceptability of lower tar cigarettes is increasing, suggesting scope for further tar reduction, although the smoking of high yielding roll your own products is increasing and should be monitored.

ii)   **Nicotine**:- The principal harmful attribute of nicotine is its addictiveness, which maintains the smoking habit, and thresholds of addiction have been postulated. Modest reductions in nicotine yields are unlikely to prevent addic-tion. It is considered extremely important, therefore, to continue to discour-age young people from experimenting with cigarettes in order to prevent addiction occurring. Although limiting nicotine to non-addictive levels to pre-vent new smokers from becoming addicted is appealing it is unlikely to be practical. Most existing smokers are addicted to nicotine and drastic reduc-tions in nicotine yield may have little impact on smokers' health risks, because of compensatory smoking. Because the link between tar and smoking relat-ed diseases is clear, further reductions in tar, with a proportional decrease in nicotine, are recommended.

iii)   Further consideration of the optimum ratio of tar:nicotine is required. More information on the bioavailability, pharmacology and pharmacokinetics of nicotine and factors that influence them, such as smoke pH, is needed in order to attract attention to the possible benefits.

iv)   A programme to monitor actual uptake of nicotine in relation to changing machine yields is called for, and this could conveniently be based on cotinine measurements within the Health Survey for England.

v)   **Carbon monoxide:** The carbon monoxide yield from cigarettes has decreased over the past 25 years, but at a slower rate than that for tar. As further measures to reduce tar yields are likely to result in similar reductions in CO, no specific action is necessary. However the ratio of yields of CO to tar should be kept under review.

vi)   **Other noxa**

a.   Research suggests that NO in tobacco smoke has a detrimental effect on the physiological function of endogenous NO. Further developments in this area will be watched with interest. As with CO, tar reduction measures are likely to result in reductions in NO.

b.   Yields of carbon-derived noxa, such as PAHs and aldehydes, closely follow those of tar. Yields of nitrogen-derived noxa do not, however, and are related to the nitrate content of tobacco. These relationships should be examined in representative current brands.

c.   The role of specific other noxa in the pathogenesis of smoking-related diseases is generally unclear. However, the carcinogenic role of PAHs and the inverse relationship of carbon- and nitrate-derived noxa requires further investigation, though conducting animal studies in this field is now difficult.

vii).   **Tobacco Industry:** Dialogue with the Tobacco Industry will help clarify recent developments in tobacco cultivation and processing and cigarette design and their relationship to the production, modification and control of emissions from tobacco smoke.

References.

1. Independent Scientific Committee on Smoking and Health. *Fourth Report*. London: HMSO, 1988.

2. Department of Health. *The Health of the Nation: A Strategy for Health in England*. London: HMSO, 1992.

3. Department of Health. *Smoke-Free for Health: an action plan to achieve the health of the nation targets on smoking*. London: HMSO, 1994.

4. Wald N, Nicolaides-Bouman A. *UK Smoking Statistics*. 2nd ed. Oxford: Oxford University Press 1991; 105-50.

5. Waller R E, Froggatt P. Product Modification. *Br Med Bull* 1996; **52**: 193-204.

6. Tang J L, Morris J K, Wald N J, et al. Mortality in relation to tar yield of cigarettes. *BMJ* 1995; **311**: 1530-3.

7. Parish S, Collins R, Peto R, et al. Cigarette smoking, tar yields, and non-fatal myocardial infarction: 14,000 cases and 32,000 controls in the United Kingdom. *BMJ* 1995; **311**: 471-7.

8. Frost C, Fullerton F M, Stephen A M, et al. The tar reduction study: randomised trial of the effect of cigarette tar yield on compensatory smoking. *Thorax* 1995; **50**: 1038-43.

9. OPCS General Household Survey 1992 London: HMSO, 1994 (table 4.20).

10. Darrall K G & Figgins J A. Roll-your-own smoke yields: theoretical and practical aspects. *Tobacco Control*. [In press].

11. Heuknes A. *Analysis of Hazardous Substances in Rolling Tobacco: report from the National Council on Tobacco and Health*, Oslo, 1994.

12. Independent Scientific Committee on Smoking and Health. *Third Report*. London: HMSO, 1983.

13. Hoffman D. Nicotine, a tobacco-specific precursor for carcinogens. In: N. Wald, P. Froggatt, eds. *Nicotine, smoking and the low tar programme*. Oxford: Oxford University Press 1989; 24-40.

14. Benowitz N L. Pharmacokinetic considerations in understanding nicotine dependence. In: *The biology of nicotine dependence*. Chichester: John Wiley and Sons, 1990; 186-209.

15. Benowitz N L, Henningfield J E. Establishing a nicotine threshold for addiction. *New England J Med*. 1994; **331**: 123-5.

16. OPCS. Health Survey for England, 1993. London: HMSO, 1995. (Office of Population Censuses & Surveys; series HS, no3).

17. Jarvis M J, Tunstall-Pedoe H, Feyerabend C, et al. Comparison of tests used to distin-guish smokers from non-smokers. *Am J Public Health* 1987; **77**: 1435-8.

18.   World Health Organization.   *Air Quality Guidelines for Europe.*   Copenhagen: WHO,1987, 210-20. (European series; no 23).

19.   Kharitonov S A, Robbins R A, Yates D, et al.   Acute and chronic effects of cigarette smoking on exhaled nitric oxide.   *Am J Respir Crit Care Med* 1995; **152**: 609-12.

20.   Phillips G F, Waller R E.   Yields of tar and other smoke components from UK cigarettes.   *Fd Chem Toxic* 1991; **29**: 469-74.

21.   Wynder EL, Hoffmann D.   Specific reduction in tumorigenic activity.   In: E L Wynder, D Hoffman, eds.   *Tobacco and tobacco smoke.* New York: Academic Press, 1967; 516-35.

22.   Royal College of Physicians.   *Smoking and health now.* London: Pitman Medical & Scientific, 1971; 52.

11. During the 1990s machine measured nicotine yields fell more sharply than in previous years. Revised analytical methods introduced in 1990 account for part of this trend, but it is probable that control of tar yield meant it was no longer possible to maintain nicotine yield at previous levels.[5]

12. The ISCSH expressed the view that, apart from its important addictive properties, nicotine, in the doses delivered by smoking, is not thought to be harmful to a healthy individual, although it may have adverse effects on people with cardiovascular disease[12]. However, nicotine is a precursor of some of the tobacco-specific N-nitroso compounds, although the role of these substances in the development of smoking-associated cancers is unclear.[13] Nicotine may also be implicated in the deficit in birth-weight associated with smoking in pregnancy.

13. The main cause of concern about nicotine is its addictive properties. Nicotine dependent smokers seek an optimum nicotine dose and if yields are reduced are liable to compensate by smoking more cigarettes or by smoking each cigarette more intensively thus negating some of the advantages of tar reduction.[8]

14. Apart from compensatory smoking nicotine uptake is also affected by smoke quality; notably pH. The smoke from most UK manufactured cigarettes is acid, leading to deep inhalation for more effective nicotine absorption. Nicotine in the alkaline smoke associated with some continental and American brands is absorbed more effectively in the mouth and upper respiratory tract. However, deep inhalation is still required to produce the rapid pulse of nicotine to the brain associated with absorption in the lung alveoli.

15. When considering the benefit of nicotine reduction, two conflicting issues emerge. Firstly, in nicotine dependent smokers, compensatory smoking following nicotine reduction might negate some of the health advantages of further tar reductions. Secondly, as nicotine is accepted as the prime addictive agent in cigarettes, nicotine levels should fall at least as fast as tar to reduce the likelihood of addiction. This point is important for young smokers, who, although likely to continue to experiment with smoking, would be less likely to become addicted, and suffer adverse long term health effects, if nicotine yields were very low.

16. These two issues are difficult to reconcile. The yield of nicotine, as measured by a smoking machine, is not the main determinant of nicotine addiction. The bioavailability of inhaled nicotine, depth of inhalation, and the kinetics of absorption, distribution in the body, metabolism and excretion of nicotine are all important and cannot be determined or compared by a smoking machine. Experimental studies also indicate that the rapid peaks in blood nicotine levels, experienced on exposure, are important in the pharmacology and addictiveness of nicotine[14], and will not be eliminated simply by a reduction in machine-measured nicotine yields.

17. It seems logical, though conjectural, that non-addictive levels of nicotine in cigarettes exist, but there are currently limited data to show what such levels might be. The work of Benowitz[15] suggests a non-addictive level of uptake of 0.1-0.2 mg of nicotine per cigarette which would be the maximum bioavailability from cigarettes with a total content of 0.5 mg of nicotine. Some current UK low tar brands have smoking machine yields of 0.5 mg of nicotine per cigarette and below but the total nicotine content of these brands is several milligrams and thus significantly greater than the 0.5 mg suggested by Benowitz. Whether people would smoke cigarettes with "non-addictive" levels of nicotine has not been tested and they are likely to have low consumer acceptability.

DEPARTMENT OF HEALTH
DEPARTMENT OF HEALTH AND SOCIAL SERVICES, NORTHERN IRELAND
THE SCOTTISH OFFICE DEPARTMENT OF HEALTH
WELSH OFFICE

REPORT OF THE SCIENTIFIC COMMITTEE ON TOBACCO AND HEALTH

CHAIRMAN:
PROFESSOR DAVID POSWILLO

London: The Stationery Office

Applications for reproduction should be made in writing to
The Copyright Unit,
Her Majesty's Stationery Office,
St. Clements House,
2-16 Colegate, Norwich. NR3 1BQ

ISBN 0 11 322124 X

Printed in the UK for The Stationery Office
J42528, 3/98, 5673.